BREADS
OF THE WORLD

ILLUSTRATED ENCYCLOPEDIA

BREADS
OF THE WORLD

CHRISTINE INGRAM
Recipes by Jennie Shapter

LORENZ BOOKS

This edition published by Lorenz Books

© 1999, 2000 Anness Publishing Limited

Lorenz Books is an imprint of
Anness Publishing Limited
Hermes House, 88-89 Blackfriars Road
London SE1 8HA

This edition distributed in Canada by Raincoast Books
8680 Cambie Street, Vancouver, British Columbia V6P 6M9

A CIP catalogue record for this book is available from the British Library

PUBLISHER: Joanna Lorenz
EXECUTIVE EDITOR: Linda Fraser
EDITOR: Susannah Blake
DESIGNER: Nigel Partridge
PHOTOGRAPHERS: Amanda Heywood and Nicki Dowey (recipes)
HOME ECONOMIST: Jennie Shapter
EDITORIAL READER: Jonathan Marshall
PRODUCTION CONTROLLER: Yolande Denny

Also published as *The World Guide to Bread* and, as part of a larger compendium, *The World Encyclopedia of
Bread and Bread Making*

Printed and bound in China

1 3 5 7 9 10 8 6 4 2

NOTES
For all recipes, quantities are given in both metric and imperial measures
and, where appropriate, measures are also given in standard cups and
spoons. Follow one set, but not a mixture, because they are not
interchangeable.

Standard spoon and cup measures are level.
1 tsp = 5ml, 1 tbsp = 15ml, 1 cup = 250ml/8fl oz

Australian standard tablespoons are 20ml. Australian readers should
use 3 tsp in place of 1 tbsp for measuring small quantities of gelatine,
cornflour, salt, etc.

Medium eggs are used unless otherwise stated.

CONTENTS

INTRODUCTION

There is something undeniably special about bread. The flavour of a good loaf, the texture of the soft crumb contrasting with the crispness of the crust, is almost a sensual experience. Who can walk home with a fresh baguette without slowly, almost absent-mindedly breaking off pieces to eat en route? Or resist the promise of a slice of a soft white farmhouse loaf, spread with butter? Most people have their own favourite: ciabatta, rich with olive oil; dark, malty rye; honeyed *challah* or a Middle Eastern bread, freshly baked and redolent of herbs and spices. Whatever the shape or texture, bread has a special place in our affections.

Even today, when bread is taken largely for granted, seen as an accompaniment for other foods, we still have a sense of its supreme significance. In some languages the word "bread" means "food", and in certain of the more rural parts of Spain and Italy, for example, you may find that bread is blessed or kissed before being broken or eaten. There are numerous rituals and traditions attached to bread. Slashing the dough with a cross or making a sign of the Cross over the loaf before baking was believed to let the devil out. Cutting the bread at both ends was also recommended to rid the house of the

ABOVE: Just a few of the many shapes and sizes of baguette available.

devil. One custom, sin-eating, was practised at funerals, where someone would eat a loaf of bread and by so doing would take on the sins of the dead person.

The obvious explanation for bread's importance is that until quite recently, it was for many quite literally the "staff of life" – the single essential food. Today, most people have more varied diets. Potatoes, pasta and rice are all enjoyed in the West and are important staple foods, but in some countries, for example France and Italy, bread is easily the most popular of the carbohydrates, eaten with every meal and in many cases with every course.

Like wine tasters, true aficionados taste bread *au naturel* in order to savour its unique taste and texture, unadulterated by other flavours. Good as this can be, the best thing about bread is that it goes so well with other foods. Throughout Europe bread is most frequently cut or broken into pieces to be eaten with a meal – to mop up soups and sauces or to eat with hams, pâtés and cheeses. Dark rye breads, spread with strongly flavoured cheese or topped with smoked fish, are popular in northern Europe, and in the Middle East breads are split and stuffed with meats and salads – a tradition that has been warmly embraced in the West too. In Britain and the USA, the European cus-

tom of serving bread with a meal, with or instead of potatoes or rice, is catching on, but sandwiches are probably still the favourite way of enjoying bread. Sandwiches have been going strong for a couple of hundred years – invented, it is said, by John Montagu, 4th Earl of Sandwich, so that he could eat a meal without having to leave the gaming table. Although baguettes and bagels are naturally ideally suited for linking bread with meat, the sandwich, clearly an English concept, is unique and continues to be the perfect vehicle for fillings that become more and more adventurous.

BREADS OF TODAY

Figures show that throughout Europe bread consumption declined after World War II. Until then it was the single most important food in the diet, but due to increased prosperity, which meant a wider choice of other foods, and mass production, which led to bread becoming increasingly insipid and tasteless, people moved away from their "daily bread". The situation was more noticeable in some

BELOW: Bagels can be filled with a variety of ingredients and make the perfect alternative to a sandwich.

BELOW: Rye breads are popular all over northern Europe and are delicious topped with smoked fish.

countries than others. In France, Italy and Spain, where people continued to demand the best, eating of bread did not decline so sharply. In Britain, however, most bread was notoriously bland – the ubiquitous white sliced loaf being little more than a convenient shape for the toaster. In supermarkets, certainly, there was a time, not so long ago, when apart from the standard pre-wrapped white loaf, the only baked goods on sale were croissants and a selection of fruited teabreads, vaguely labelled as "Continental". Yet within the last ten years, things have improved by leaps and bounds. Perhaps supermarkets, finding that the smell of freshly baked bread enticed shoppers into their stores, installed more in-store bakeries. Or perhaps shoppers who travelled abroad and sampled the breads of other countries created a demand for better breads made with better flours, using more imaginative recipes and untreated with additives.

Nowadays there is a huge choice of breads available both from independent bakeries and from the large supermarkets. Italian ciabatta and focaccia are now a regular sight, even in the smallest food stores, as are the various Spanish, Indian and Middle Eastern breads. There is an increasingly interesting choice of German, Danish, Scandinavian and eastern European breads and, among the French breads, there is now a truly good range on offer. If the supermarket has an in-store bakery, baguettes are likely to be freshly baked and some are now as good as the real thing. The availability of *pain de campagnes*, *levains* and other rustic breads means that you can choose breads to suit the style of meal you are serving, while sweet breads, such as brioches and croissants from France, *pane al cioccolato* from Italy and numerous offerings from Germany mean that there is much more to choose from than simply toast at breakfast and malt loaf at tea time.

Local bakers, although competing with the supermarkets, have paradoxically benefited from the range on offer at supermarkets. The more breads there are available, the more people feel inclined to try other baked goods. Small bakers, who

BELOW: French brioches make a wonderful change from toast at breakfast.

could easily have lost customers to the big stores, have risen to the challenge by producing their own range of country-style and fine breads. Craft bakers are producing traditional breads, at the same time experimenting with recipes they have devised themselves. Bread making has never been a tradition that stood still. The best craft bakers have ensured that bread making has continued to evolve, resulting in the emergence of all sorts of corn and barley breads, mixed-grain loaves and a range of new sourdoughs.

Added to this are the many European-style bakeries. Set up and run by émigrés from all parts of Europe and beyond,

BELOW: Italian Pane al Cioccolato *is studded with dark chocolate chunks and is often served with creamy mascarpone cheese as a snack.*

these bakeries are the best source of many of the most authentic European breads. In supermarkets you will invariably find ciabatta or focaccia, but for *pagnotta* or *pane sciocco* you are likely to need an Italian baker, who will be only too happy to provide you with the loaves and tell you all about them.

Once you have found a bakery you like, there are no particular tips for buying bread; the baker will be pleased to explain the different styles of loaves and advise on their keeping qualities. Crusty breads, such as baguettes, round cobs or Italian country loaves, are known as "oven bottom" or "oven bottom-baked", which means they have been baked, without tins or containers, on the sole of the oven or on flat sheet trays. They are evenly crusty, although the type of dough, the humidity during proving, the steam in the oven and the heat itself determines whether the crust is fragile or chewy. Loaves, such as the English farmhouse, baked in metal tins, characteristically have a golden top, but with thinner crusts on the sides. Rolls or breads baked up against each other have even softer sides and are described as "batch-baked". Sourdough breads are made without yeast – using a natural leaven instead – and are often labelled as "yeast-free" breads or "naturally leavened". There are many varieties, some made entirely from wheat, some from rye, others from a blend of both. They are normally heavier than an average loaf, with a dense texture and pleasantly tart flavour.

HISTORY

Bread seems to be a recurring theme in history. Most people could be forgiven for thinking that history was driven by great scientists and ambitious men. But look closer and you will find that the incentive behind many of our greatest inventions was the availability, production and delivery of food – our "daily bread" in the widest terms. The wheel, the plough and the windmill right through to steam and motorization all plot a course that was concerned specifically with agriculture and producing food. Similarly, the aspirations of any king or queen were intimately connected with the feeding of their people. The poorer and hungrier the population, the more insecure was their ruler's position. "Give them bread and circuses!" said Juvenal in the 1st century AD, referring to the Roman mob, in a constant state of unrest because of poverty and starvation; and Queen Marie Antoinette famously said "Let them eat cake", on being told that the peasants were rioting because they had no bread. Almost all revolutions came about because of famine, and bread was the single food that might alone have averted such an event.

THE FIRST BREAD

Archaeology and history show that bread has been eaten since the earliest times. Remains of stone querns indicate that cereal was ground in prehistoric Britain to make a branny-type grain. It is likely that this would have been fashioned into

ABOVE: Distributing bread to the poor in Paris after the famine in 1662.

cakes and cooked over an open fire to make a coarse flat cake. At the same time in Egypt, where civilization was considerably more advanced, bread was a regular part of daily life and indeed the Egyptians are credited with being the first people to make bread. Paintings on the walls of tombs depict bread being offered to the gods and the flat oval-shaped breads look uncannily like *aiysh*, the Egyptian bread still eaten today. Other pictures show round or cone-shaped breads and it is likely that they were all leavened, since the water from the Nile contains the same strain of yeast that is used in baking today. The Greeks initially made unleavened breads, but during the last millennium BC leavens were introduced to raise their breads and the loaves were baked in bread ovens. Once wheat flour replaced barley meal, the Greeks became very partial to bread, their bakers producing a huge range of different breads made with honey or milk or sprinkled with sesame or poppy seed, according to one account written in the 1st century AD.

Elsewhere, the leavening of bread became commonplace, even if at first it might have come about by accident. Natural yeasts exist in the air around us and a warm paste of flour and water will

BELOW: By the 1st century AD, Roman bakers had perfected their craft, as this mural shows..

ABOVE: Throughout Europe, windmills were built to make milling easier.

spontaneously start to ferment if left for a couple of hours, so leavened bread is probably almost as ancient as the unleavened cakes baked over hot stones. Sourdoughs made by this natural method became popular in many parts of Europe, and the traditions continue to this day with sourdough ryes from eastern Europe and Germany, wheaten *levains* such as *pain de campagne* and Italian country loaves from more southerly regions.

In ancient Britain, about the time of the Roman invasion, beer barm – the yeasty froth on fermenting liquor – began to be used as a leaven. Barley was by far the most important crop at that time and ale was widely brewed. Once the use of natural leavens had become widespread, it would have been but a small step to realize that beer barm, with the same sweet/sour smell, could be used as well.

In Biblical times, leavened bread was common. In the Book of Genesis, Lot, the son of Abraham, welcomes two angels to his house and "baked for them unleavened bread", which suggests that leavened

bread was the more usual food for non-angels. Today, Jews bake unleavened bread – *matzos* – for Passover, in remembrance of the Hebrews' escape from Egypt, and unleavened bread is frequently the bread for ritual or sacred occasions.

Bread also plays a central role in Christianity. Jesus fed the five thousand

BELOW: The original bread ovens were often made of fireproof stone or bricks.

with bread, and at the last supper he broke unleavened bread (it being Passover), giving thanks to the Lord and literally identifying with it, with the words "this is my body", the act of which is recalled in every Christian Mass.

BREAD IN BRITAIN AND EUROPE DURING THE MIDDLE AGES

The Romans brought wheat, oats and rye to Britain along with many of their bread-making techniques. However, while for a time bread making became more sophisticated, it suffered a setback once the Romans had left. During the Dark Ages, the growing and harvesting of cereal and then the making and baking of bread would have been a hit-or-miss affair. Families would have gathered cereals from their local fields and threshed the grain either in their own home or by using a quern stone belonging to the village.

By the Middle Ages, however, horses had begun to be used for ploughing and cultivation began to be more organized. The watermill and then the windmill were invented, probably first in England and then elsewhere in Europe. Perhaps this was something of a mixed blessing, for while the mill certainly took the backache out of the task, the lord of the manor retained rights over the mill and would oblige the serfs who worked his land to pay a tithe for the use of the mill. To add insult to injury, the bakehouse, often adjoining the mill, also made a charge to the families who used it and in a period when cottages were flimsy constructions without ovens or even chimneys, families often had little option but to take their bread to the communal oven.

The loaves themselves were normally huge, weighing more than 4.5kg/10lb, and would be expected to feed the family for several days. Made of a mixture of grain – wheat, barley, millet and rye – they would have been coarse mealy loaves. If the winters were not too harsh, the summers warm and the rainfall neither too great nor too little, harvests would be good and people could survive on a diet of bread, ale and pottage (a stew made of pulses and meat). However, after a poor harvest, cereal became scarce and people would have to use almost anything that could be ground to a meal. Acorns and roots were often the stand-bys in times of famine in Europe, while in England the poor would have to resort to horse bread, a type of mealy cake made of ground beans, so-called as it was normally fed to animals.

BELOW: In 15th-century France a flattish bread was cooked over an open fire.

ABOVE: This 16th-century bake-house in Scandinavia was built next door to a public bath – perhaps the oven also warmed the water.

In 1266 laws were introduced in England, known as the Assizes of Bread, which regulated that the weight of bread should be fixed to a certain price. For the price of one penny it was set down that three types of bread should be available: white loaves made from bolted (sifted) flour, which were the lightest breads, wheaten loaves made of more coarsely sifted meal and weighing half as much again, and finally the household loaf, the heaviest of all three and made of unrefined meal. The Assize system was deeply unpopular with bakers, but it nevertheless continued for some 450 years, which testifies to the importance the government attached to bread being available and affordable for the whole population.

BRITAIN IN TUDOR TIMES

Bread and pottage continued to be the staple foods for most people of England under the Tudors, and while the wealthier people could afford a more varied diet, bread was still the most important food at the table. All large households baked their own bread and bread also became available from bakeries which sprang up in most towns. These professional bakers would bake some customers' loaves for them, in addition to making and selling their own, although most breads by this time were baked at home, normally over a hearth, since an open oven continued to be a considerable fire risk.

For the poor, most bread was made of a mixture of grains, which would vary depending on the part of the country: rye in Norfolk; barley in north-west England and the lowlands of Scotland, Wales and Cornwall; and oats in the uplands of Wales and the Scottish Highlands. For the poorest, a mixed grain called maslin was often used, while peasant bread made from peas and beans continued to be made during severe hardship.

Although the more affluent people did eat plain brown bread, they also began to acquire a liking for white bread. White bread was considered superior for several reasons: it was more expensive, owing to the time and effort required to sift out the bran, and it implied prestige; added to which the Church used a white bread called Pandemain, by definition more refined, as the sacramental bread. People took this to mean better, and white bread acquired a cachet which has only really been dented in the last 20 years.

Known by various names, this white bread eventually came to be known as manchet. Manchets were made from the finest wheat flour and were relatively small, sometimes not much bigger than a large roll; compared with the large plain breads, they were not considered sufficient for one person at a meal.

Another common practice, dating from the Middle Ages and surviving until the end of the 16th century, was the use of trenchers. These were thick slices of bread from large four-day-old wholemeal loaves, which served as plates for both the less affluent and the wealthy, hard-baked for the purpose and cut into squares or oblongs. The custom was also practised in

France, and trencher breads were made in Corbeil and sold in the markets of Paris. Meat and fish would be placed on top of each slice, the bread soaking up any gravy. Those who were still hungry would then eat their trencher – from where we get the expression "trencherman", someone renowned for the amount he eats. In wealthy families it would have been unseemly to eat the trencher, not to say unnecessary, as there would have been sufficient food offered at table. Instead, the servants would take the pieces of bread and give them to the almshouses.

LATER CENTURIES

Within the British Isles and across Europe, the lot of the peasant farmer contrasted sharply with that of the wealthy. During the 18th century the price of wheat rose steeply. In Britain, the Corn Laws, which were largely responsible for the price increases, were finally repealed in 1846. In France, the State's failure to respond to the crisis resulted in revolution. Around this time, the potato – introduced to Europe at the beginning of the 17th century – finally gained acceptance. In France and the south of England, wheat continued to be the favoured staple, but potatoes were used increasingly and by the middle of the 19th century, potatoes were as much a staple as bread. For the poor, bread and potatoes together formed the basis of a meagre diet. In Ireland, however, potatoes were often the only food, resulting in the catastrophic famine of the 1840s when potato blight struck.

BELOW: Most affluent homes had a built-in oven, fired by wood or peat.

ABOVE: In Victorian times all large households baked their own bread.

BAKING METHODS

The first means of baking or cooking a bread was simply by placing the dough on a heated stone over the dying embers of a fire. This technique is not dissimilar to that used today by the Australian bushmen when making their damper bread. The first English settlers in Virginia also used the same principle for their maize breads, baking the dough over hot ashes or in hot sand. The advantage is that no hardware or utensils are required; the disadvantage is that the bread, even if leavened, is mainly flat. At some point someone came up with the idea of placing a pot over the bread. The steamy heat caused the bread to rise and variations on this theme continued for hundreds of years among poorer people.

At the same time, most villages had a bakehouse, either attached to the mill or owned by the baker. Farmers and larger households often had their own bread ovens, fired with wood and furze (gorse). Although these fuels were cheap to collect, lighting and heating the oven would have been a time-consuming process and for most households it would be lit only once a week. After the week's bread had been baked, biscuits and cakes, which required lower temperatures, would be placed in the cooling oven.

Originally, ovens were heated using wood that was burnt on the oven floor. Once the oven was hot, the embers were removed using a long-handled tool, called a peel. These ancient ovens were built of fire-proof stone, and later replaced by bricks. The stone or bricks would become white hot and then very gradually the heat would decrease as the bread was baked. Flat breads, such as the Italian *focaccia*, would have been the first breads to go into these immensely hot ovens, where they would be baked quickly and crisply. Larger loaves would then be baked, the slowly decreasing heat ensuring that the bread had a good thick crust, which meant that it kept well for the days ahead.

In the USA, Australia, Britain, France and other parts of Europe, enthusiasts have restored these wood-burning ovens and their bread, which is made to traditional recipes, is quite delicious.

In Ireland, bread was cooked in a type of Dutch oven, which was set in peat with burning embers piled around it. A similar type of oven is still used by the people of Dutch ancestry in South Africa, who make their pot bread by baking it in a cast-iron pot piled high with smouldering embers.

BREADS OF THE WORLD

Bread is a particularly fundamental aspect of a country's cuisine – it reflects the climate and geography, as well as the customs, culture and religious beliefs of the people. This comprehensive guide includes the world's best-loved breads and many less well-known loaves, too. It will help you recognize the different breads that are sold in supermarkets and bakeries, act as a guide if you are travelling abroad, and encourage you to sample local breads, whether you've travelled halfway across the world, or simply moved to a new area.

BRITISH BREADS

British bread is now considered as good as any bread from Europe, something that could not have been said 20, or even 10 years ago. In the 1970s and 80s British holiday-makers discovered the delights of French baguettes, Italian ciabatta and all the other wonderful breads of Europe, and began asking why their own bread was so uninteresting. Many small bakers, of course, had been producing excellent bread for years, a delight for their customers but unknown to all those who shopped mostly in supermarkets. Things changed when supermarkets introduced their own in-store bakeries. Suddenly fresh bread was easily and readily available. The equation was simple. Fresh bread tasted great; people started eating more of it, and thus more bread, and in greater diversity, was made and sold. It's an equation where everyone gains. Bread is relatively cheap; it's an excellent food; it can be eaten with almost any meal and there is now a huge choice for the consumer. Small bakers have risen to the challenge of the supermarkets by producing their own speciality breads. All sorts of sourdoughs, ryes and corn breads are now available, along with a vast range of the more traditional British breads. The following breads are among the better known shapes, and are the breads you are

RIGHT: A bloomer can be distinguished by the diagonal slashes across the top

likely to find in almost any good bakery and in most supermarkets, too. White breads are defined by their shape rather than the dough, and the majority of loaves are made using the same dough. However, once you start tasting and comparing breads, you will discover that the shape, the method of cooking and even the amount of slashing on the loaf will alter the flavour.

BATCHED BREAD

These loaves are baked together without tins so that there are no crusts along the sides, the individual loaves being broken apart when baked. The top crust is normally soft. Brick or sister brick loaves are two loaves baked together in large square or rectangular tins and then broken apart to give a half-batched effect.

BLOOMER

This is a popular oven bottom-baked loaf, i.e. one that is baked without a tin, either on a tray or on the sole of the oven. It has a plump, oval shape and is distinguished by five or six diagonal slashes across the upper crust. A bloomer from a good baker's has a soft crumb and a fragile and sharp crust. However, shop-bought bloomers that have been pre-wrapped in plastic often have a disappointingly flabby crust. Bloomers can be made

ABOVE: Batched loaves are not necessarily uniform in shape, but always have soft sides. White and brown loaves are available.

ABOVE: Cornmeal loaf (top) and brown and white cobs. The even texture of the crumb on the cob loaves means that they make excellent toast.

using brown wheat flour, rye or multigrain; however, the most popular type is white.

COB

The cob is perhaps the oldest and most basic of British loaves. The loaf is round and completely plain without slashes or decoration, and is oven-baked and crusty. The word "cob" is an old English word for a head, and plain round loaves made with coarse, brown meal would have been the basic loaf for many families for genera-

tions. Cobs today can be white, but are usually brown, wholemeal or Granary.

COBURG

This white, round, oven bottom-baked loaf has a cross slash on the upper crust, distinguishing it from the cob. Some bakers slash the loaf before the final rising to produce a wide-spread loaf with four clover-leaf corners. Others slash more conservatively for a loaf that retains its basic round shape.

PAN COBURG

This loaf is baked in a shallow round tin, the diagonally slashed crust rising up and over the sides of the tin to look a bit like a

cauliflower, a name by which it is also known. Specialist craft bakers sometimes make this loaf, either on order or because they have an appreciative clientele, but it is a popular bread to make at home.

CHEQUERBOARD

Also known as a porcupine or rumpy loaf, this bread is cross-hatched to give a "chequerboard" crust. The loaf is usually floured before being cut, and the deeper the cuts, the more the crust will spread.

CORNMEAL

This is not a traditional British loaf, but is becoming increasingly popular, especially among some of the small craft bakers who have developed their own recipes, blending cornmeal with a strong white or wholemeal flour. Sometimes whole corn kernels are also added to give a delicious loaf with good texture.

DANISH

A traditional – or proper – Danish loaf is a round loaf with one central lengthways cut. Originally oven bottom-baked to give a good crust, it was always made using white flour – unlike the cobs and coburgs

RIGHT: A good Danish loaf should have a floury, but firm crust and a fairly dense crumb.

BELOW: Hovis loaves come in various sizes but all have the familiar tin shape with "Hovis" on the sides.

which would have used the cheaper and more widely available brown meal. Danish loaves today, however, are as likely to be more oval in shape. A good Danish from a bakery still has the firm crust and is cut with frequent and deep diagonal slashes on the top. A common supermarket version of a Danish is a pre-wrapped, cylindrical sliced loaf that is distinguished mainly by the lightness of the crumb. Although this is advertised as virtue, there is very little that can be said in its favour, since it is bland to the extent of being quite tasteless. So, whenever possible, buy from your baker instead.

FARMHOUSE LOAF

Farmhouse tins are shallow and somewhat squat, producing the characteristic plump tin loaves. At

RIGHT: Plaits can be elaborate. Most are enriched with eggs and butter.

one time special bread tins were used, which impressed the word "Farmhouse" along the side of the loaf. This was a fashion introduced towards the end of the last century when there was a move away from the "whiter-than-white" breads that had become immensely popular, to a more healthy bread. The original farmhouse loaves were made using a brown flour to satisfy the instincts of the more health conscious, although ironically today most farmhouse loaves are white. Today some craft bakers make their own special farmhouse breads using a dough that has been fermented for longer than usual, but the majority of farmhouse loaves are made using exactly the same dough as other white breads. The difference, as is often the case, is in the shape.

HOVIS

No sooner had the poor in Britain been converted to the values and merits of white bread, than a movement began to persuade people that breads containing wheat germ, the bits discarded by the roller mills, were highly valuable nutritionally. A flour was developed that put the wheat germ back into the flour, after first stabilizing it to prevent rancidity. The flour was called Hovis (from the Latin *hominis vis*, meaning "the life of man") and one of the most enduring proprietary breads was born. All Hovis loaves, whether baked at home or bought from a bakery, are made using Hovis flour, although there are a variety of different mixes, some containing more of the wholemeal along with other

grains. Hovis loaves have their name impressed along the side and some are quite delicious. Pre-packed and sliced loaves have less character.

INNES

Innes Original is one of the few sourdough loaves widely available in Britain today, although individual bakers may well make their own favourite sourdough.

PLAIT

Specialist bakers often produce their own plaited loaves, which can be made from anything between three and eight strands of dough. They mimic the popular European and Jewish breads but are no less British for all that, having been made by craft bakers for generations. They are normally white and can be crusty, made using plain dough, or they can be enriched with butter, eggs and milk and are therefore soft.

SPIRAL

Several of the European breads are shaped by rolling the dough into a sausage shape and then twisting it around to make a spiral or snail shape. Specialist bakers may produce their own particular favourite, which may be white and crusty or enriched and sprinkled with poppy seeds or glazed with egg.

ABOVE: A spiral loaf

RIGHT: Ground nuts give this walnut bread a slightly beige colour.

WALNUT BREAD

There are two styles of British walnut loaf, though the French *pain aux noix* is more commonly available. The white bloomer-shaped walnut loaf contains coarsely ground walnuts while the walnut Granary is made using larger chunks of walnut. Both are fairly soft loaves with an airy texture.

OPPOSITE: The white farmhouse loaf produced today (top) is somewhat squat in shape with a characteristic central slash. Wholemeal and Granary loaves (left and right) can be tin-baked or oven bottom-baked.

BELOW: The obvious choice for making sandwiches is the eponymous sandwich loaf, but any tin or split tin loaf works well, despite the more irregular shape.

TIN/SPLIT TIN LOAVES

These loaves are baked in tins, the crust either forming a domed shape (tin), or being slashed along the centre before baking (split tin), so that there is a larger crust area. The crust is normally fairly soft, particularly on loaves that have been pre-packed. A sandwich loaf, which is baked in a completely enclosed tin, is – as the name suggests – popular for making sandwiches since all the slices are conveniently square.

VITBE

Like Hovis, this is another loaf made from a proprietary brand of flour, which also returns the stabilized wheat germ to the white flour. There are several VitBe loaves: the original wheat germ bread and a Hi-Bran loaf.

VIENNA BATONS

A Vienna baton is a slashed long loaf which was, until very recently, the British approximation of the French baguette. The crumb is light and airy, the crust crisp and flaky.

The French baguette was developed partly from a process that originated in Vienna where steam was injected into the oven. Known as the "Vienna" technique, the process was adopted by British bakers in the forlorn hope of reproducing the increasingly popular baguette. The experiment wasn't entirely successful. Vienna batons resemble baguettes only in shape. Their light airy crumb and crisp flaky crust nevertheless have a character of their own and they are surprisingly good, sliced, topped with grated cheese, then toasted and added to French onion soup.

ENGLISH BREADS

ENGLISH OATMEAL BREAD

Oats have always been an important crop in England and other parts of the British Isles, although mainly for animal feed. Oatmeal contains no gluten, so breads made entirely using oats were inevitably flat, baked on stones or on a griddle. Many parts of England, as well as Wales and Scotland, have their own traditional oatmeal cakes, but the meal can be used for baking loaves if it is mixed with wheat flour.

CORNISH SAFFRON CAKE

This Cornish sweet bread is yeast-leavened, enriched with fruit and spiced with nutmeg, cinnamon and saffron. Saffron was an important crop in England in the 16th century and although it gradually declined, it continued to survive in the West Country, where numerous traditional breads and cakes include the tiny strands of saffron, adding a delicate flavour and pretty colouring.

LEFT: An English favourite – cottage loaf

BELOW: Cornish saffron cake is one of the best known of the English currant breads.

COTTAGE LOAF

The cottage loaf must be among the oldest shapes of English breads. The distinctive arrangement of a smallish round loaf baked on top of a larger round loaf seems to be a peculiarity to England and Elizabeth David in her *English Bread and Yeast Cookery* suggests that it might have originated as an improvised way of economizing on baking space in a small oven. The two loaves are wedded together by pushing a wooden spoon handle or fingers down the centre of the two rounds and sometimes the sides are snipped to give an extra crusty finish. Traditionally, cottage loaves would have been baked on the floor of the oven and the best cottage loaves today have a thick, dark bottom crust. Sadly, few high-street bakers have the time or oven space for these celebrated loaves and they are not widely available. For special occasions or on request, some of the smaller specialist bakers will bake a cottage loaf and, no doubt, take great pleasure in doing so.

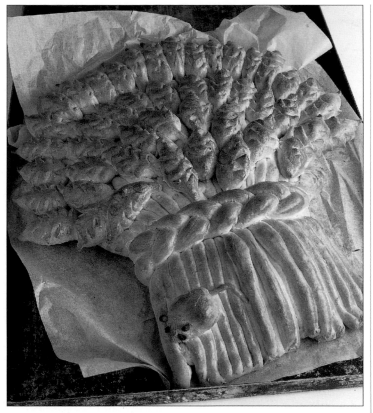

ABOVE: A harvest loaf gives bakers an opportunity to practise their skill and can be quite spectacular.

GUERNSEY GÂCHE

From this small British island off the coast of Normandy come two breads that are both known as "gâche". The French, brioche-style gâche is highly spiced with cloves and made in proper Normandy style with apples. The British version is heavier, enriched with candied peel and sultanas, and made with eggs and rich Guernsey butter and milk.

HARVEST LOAF

Harvest loaves are not really intended for eating but are made by bakers in the autumn to coincide with harvest festivals in churches and schools. It is a tradition that has happily endured in many of the smaller villages of England and bakers clearly enjoy the opportunity to demonstrate their skill and expertise.

HOT CROSS BUNS

Small yeasted buns have been popular in England since medieval times. Small breads, enriched with eggs, currants and raisins and spiced with nutmeg and cinnamon, were served to accompany wine at the end of a feast. They became a particular Lent favourite among the Elizabethans, who enjoyed displaying their wealth and sophistication by using

CRUMPETS

Crumpets are another traditional bread, and are similar to pikelets and muffins. Recipes for crumpets date from the 18th century and then, just as now, they were always toasted and eaten with lashings of butter. Today, crumpets are made using yeast and baking powder (or bicarbonate of soda and cream of tartar), which accounts for their characteristic holey surface. Crumpets are widely available pre-packed from supermarkets but the superior crumpets from specialist bakers are harder to find and it might be simpler in the long run to make your own.

ABOVE: Crumpets are traditionally served warm with butter.

the expensive and much sought-after spices from the Far East. During the Middle Ages it was common practice to mark loaves with a deep cross before baking to ward off evil spirits and, although the custom was abandoned after the Reformation as being popish, the buns made for Good Friday continued the custom for this most significant of religious days. Hot cross buns are now available almost all year round. They normally make an appearance shortly after Christmas so the significance of Easter and the pleasure of enjoying food according to the season, like so many things, is but a distant memory. Small bakers, however, continue to bake their own hot cross buns only during Lent and most have the attraction of not being so horribly over-spiced.

LEFT: Hot cross buns are the traditional Easter treat.

LARDY CAKE

There are many different versions of this unequivocally English bread, but all go by the same name and all are very rich. Originally, lardy cakes were made for celebrations, notably harvest festivals, but as sugar and fruit became more affordable they became popular all year round. Various English counties lay claim to lardy cake. You can certainly eat delicious lardy cake in Lancashire and Yorkshire, and Northumberland, too, has its own speciality. The Midlands and Derbyshire are partial to a very sweet variety, while further south, in Surrey and Hampshire, there are versions of fruitless lardy cakes. The round, flattish breads are made using a basic white dough, which is layered with fat, sugar and fruit. Lardy cake, almost by definition, is very calorific (so be warned) and it contains pork lard and is therefore a prohibited food for vegetarians. The cake is still often sold by weight or by the piece.

ABOVE: A sticky, rich and tasty lardy cake

RIGHT: Lincolnshire plum bread makes a pleasant tea-time treat, spread with butter or damson jelly.

LINCOLNSHIRE PLUM BREAD

Just as with plum pudding or plum cake, plum means dried fruit in this context, namely currants, raisins and sultanas. There are several of these plum breads – fruited breads – sold in supermarkets, distributed by a variety of producers. However, the Lincolnshire plum bread seems to be the best known. This, too, is widely available but visitors to Lincolnshire should try if possible to sample the non-commercial version, as baked by smaller specialist bakers.

MUFFINS

English muffins – to give them their correct name and to differentiate them from American muffins, which resemble English fairy cakes – belong to the same tradition as crumpets, although there are several differences, as enthusiasts would be only too keen to point out. Like crumpets, they are a part of an English folk memory that includes the muffin man, winter afternoons in front of the fire, toasting forks and tea time. Although muffins and crumpets are made from the same, or similar, basic recipes, muffins use a stiffer mixture and are consequently thicker with a thin skin or crust on each side and without the characteristic holes of crumpets. Like crumpets, muffins are delicious toasted, either split and then toasted or toasted and then split (it makes a difference!) and served with butter. Pre-packed muffins are available in any supermarket. Bakers also occasionally make their own. (Look out for those made by small craft bakeries, which are likely to have a better flavour and a crisper crust.)

BELOW: Once mostly white, brown muffins are now almost as popular.

to the townspeople. The story goes that Sally Lunn, a Huguenot, brought her recipe from France and adapted it to the English oven. Alternatively, although less romantically, the word is thought to be a corruption of the French *soleil lune* or "sun and moon" cake. Either way, Sally Lunn is a distinctive-

LEFT: Pikelets are a speciality of northern England

looking bread with tall sides and a billowing top like the *kugelhopf* of Alsace. Although there is no one authorized version, Sally Lunn is always made using white flour and yeast, enriched with butter and cream. It can be lightly spiced and slightly citrusy, but should not be over-flavoured. It is often sold in cake shops, split and spread with butter or clotted cream.

SOURDOUGH

There is no tradition of making sourdoughs in England but many of the more adventurous bakers are now producing loaves using a sourdough leaven. There are all sorts of breads using various blends of wheat and rye flours, and some are made using a potato starter. Most loaves of this type are, however, flattish and fairly dense with a definite sour/acid flavour.

PIKELETS

Some people say pikelet is just another name for crumpet and in some parts of the country the words are synonymous. However, while both pikelets and crumpets have the distinctive holey tops, pikelets are not cooked in rings but are free form in shape, being cooked straight on the griddle like Scotch pancakes or the Welsh crumpets *bara pyglyd* (pronounced piglet, and from which pikelets may well get their name). The mixture for pikelets is very much the same as crumpets, but perhaps a bit thinner for pikelets. Bakers in the counties of Leicestershire, Derbyshire, Yorkshire and Lancashire may produce them on a regular basis, and they are sometimes available from larger supermarkets. Otherwise you will need to find a baker who specializes in regional breads and cakes.

SALLY LUNN

This brioche-style cake is a speciality of the West Country, or more particularly Bath, where supposedly a lass called Sally Lunn once sold her cakes

ABOVE: Sally Lunn, with its delicate citrus flavour, is often sliced into three layers and filled with clotted cream

BELOW: Sourdough

STOTTIE

This flattish bread is native to the north-east of England, where it is widely available, although almost unheard of anywhere else. Almost always white, it is flat with a soft, floury crust, often (but not always) scored with a single slash or cross. Local bakers explain that stotties were traditionally the last things to be baked in the oven at the end of the day, the name itself coming from the local word "stott", meaning to throw to the ground. The bread apparently was ready for eating if it rebounded from the floor! Stottie bread (perhaps as a result of such bad treatment) is rather dry with an open crumb and fairly chewy texture. It is, however, delicious with another regional dish, ham and pease pudding (based on split peas).

STAFFORDSHIRE OATCAKES

Unlike the small, crumbly Scottish oatcake, Staffordshire oatcakes are soft and floppy and are the size of small pancakes. They are known locally as "turnstall tortillas" and they are indeed similar to a tortilla, although unlike the Mexican bread, these are eaten in true English fashion with eggs and bacon for breakfast or butter and honey for tea.

The oatcakes are made from a mixture of oatmeal and flour, yeast and milk or water. It is likely that they have been made in Staffordshire for centuries, as all sorts of oatcakes and griddle cakes were common in the North of England from Tudor times. With the Industrial Revolution though, they became associated with the Staffordshire potteries and while available from many supermarkets, the best are those that are baked on the premises of local bakers in places such as Stoke-on-Trent.

YORKSHIRE FARL

This is a round soda bread, similar to the Irish soda breads, that is cross-slashed into quarters (farls) before being baked.

BELOW: Stotties are a favourite in the north of England.

WELSH BREADS

BARA BRITH

Bara brith is one of the best-known fruit breads of the British Isles. "Bara" is the Welsh word for bread, while "brith", meaning spotted, describes the currants that are an essential ingredient. Although there are brown or "wholemeal" versions, bara brith is normally made using white flour. A good bara brith is yeast-leavened, lightly spiced and fairly dense in texture. Today, raisins and mixed peel are often added, but currants are the essential ingredient and bakers in Wales will commonly plump these first in cold tea, perhaps to emulate the juicy blackcurrants thought to have been the original fruit in bara brith. The bread is sold in most large supermarkets and some delicatessens, but for a really traditional bara brith you may need to travel to Wales, where there are many different versions from which you can choose your own particular favourite.

RIGHT: Bara brith was considered a luxury loaf when dried fruit was expensive. It is still one of the most delicious teabreads.

WELSH COB

Unlike the round English cob, a Welsh cob is something like a cross between an English farmhouse and a stottie. It is baked oven crusty and is normally made from white flour. Usually dusted with flour before baking, these loaves may also have a cut along the centre.

ABOVE: Welsh cob

WELSH COTTAGE

The Welsh cottage loaf, like its English equivalent, is not often made by bakers as it is time-consuming and takes up a lot of oven space. However, specialist bakers and some restaurants may produce these loaves for their customers. The bottom half of the loaf is sometimes slashed vertically before the final rising.

WELSH POT BREAD

In the days before families had ovens for baking, people improvised in the most ingenious ways. Dough, which would normally have been a fairly coarse, brown meal, would be moulded in an iron pot and then turned upside-down on to a flat stone lying over a wood-burning fire. Alternatively, the dough was baked in a three-legged pot, which also would be placed over an open fire, and smouldering peat would then have been piled on top. Pot breads like these are not made these days, but occasionally some restaurants will make their own version, using earthenware pots to create interesting and crusty loaves.

LEFT: Welsh cottage

WELSH TINS

Welsh tins have a crusty appearance with a pleasant soft crumb. The white loaves are sometimes cross-hatched but are often, like the wholemeal and Granary versions, left plain. Like most tin loaves, this bread makes great toast and is often served buttered with the delicious, slightly salty Welsh butter.

LEFT: Swansea loaf, now made only rarely, was a popular bread in the 18th century.

SWANSEA LOAF

Although nowadays fairly rare, this was once the basic loaf for all who lived in Swansea and its environs. It was normally a batch-baked bread, made with a white wheat flour, and would have been sold in the markets. Some local restaurants that specialize in Welsh food may bake this bread for guests, or there are museums around Swansea that give regular exhibitions of bread making: the bread is made and baked as you watch, so that you have the opportunity of tasting it as it once really was – made by traditional methods, baked in old-fashioned ovens and served still warm.

BELOW: Left to right: white, wholemeal and Granary Welsh tin loaves

SCOTTISH BREADS

ABERDEEN BUTTERY ROWIES

Scottish bakers, especially when explaining their wares to the uninitiated, may well describe these delicious little rolls as Scottish croissants. There are certainly similarities. Although the shape differs, rowies being round or oval, they are both made in a similar way: layered with butter so they have a delicious texture that resembles pastry. Rowies, however, are lighter and more savoury than croissants, using less butter but more salt. They are widely available in Scotland, less so as you move further south.

LEFT: Despite the name, soft rolls are slightly crusty.

SELKIRK BANNOCK

This fruited loaf is popular throughout Britain and is available from most large supermarkets, although there was once a time when these breads were only made in the town of Selkirk. It is a round loaf (normally white) and, unlike barm brack and bara brith to which it is often compared, should be completely unspiced. It, too, contains fruit, some versions using only sultanas, others containing currants and candied peel as well. Traditionally it would have been made with lard, making it similar to lardy cake, but most shop-bought versions today use butter or vegetable fat instead, although some older recipes may still suggest a mixture of butter and lard.

BARLEY BANNOCK

"Bannock" is an Old English word of Celtic origin and was probably the first word used to describe bread, as long ago as the 5th century AD. The word still has a rather antiquated ring to it. It generally describes a type of flat, scone-like bread and in Scotland the two words "bannock" and "scone" are used interchangeably. Bannocks were originally unleavened breads, made with barley or oatmeal and cooked on a griddle. Such flat, dense breads are unheard of these days. Most of today's bannocks are made using baking powder or bicarbonate of soda as a raising agent, which gives them a light, airy texture. Some craft bakeries produce bannocks using a natural leaven. The sour flavour is something of an acquired taste, especially when coupled with that of the barley. The breads are still cooked on a griddle and have the characteristic earthy flavour of barley.

MELROSE LOAF

This is Scotland's best-known soda bread. It is a proprietary bread, made by a bakery in south of Scotland. It is a wholemeal, malted loaf with a dense texture and is a popular bread for breakfast, often being spread with butter and marmalade.

LEFT: Aberdeen buttery rowies

SCOTCH BREAD

Scottish bakers are renowned for their bread and these fine loaves are the most popular bread in Scotland, used for sandwiches and toast. Often simply called a "plain" loaf, the bread has the characteristic soft sides of a batch-baked loaf and the top is baked to a dark brown. It has a particularly good flavour, thanks to the longer than usual fermentation period.

MORNING ROLLS

These soft and flattish, floury rolls are to be found in every bakery and supermarket in Scotland. They are called "baps" in some parts of Scotland; in other parts such a word is completely unheard of and the rolls are called "morning rolls" or just "rolls". The product, however, is clearly the same: made with plain, rather than strong flour, the rolls can be wholemeal or brown, but are more commonly white. They are made with lard, which is rubbed into the flour. This is mixed to a dough with milk and water and, of course, yeast, creating the characteristic soft texture. The rolls are normally batched together on large baking trays and are pulled apart after cooking so, like batched bread, they have little or no side crust and are often almost square in shape. A little dimple in the centre of the roll, pressed into the dough just before baking to stop the tops blistering, is a sign of a true traditional morning

ABOVE: Scotch bread is mostly used for sandwiches.

roll but these marks frequently disappear in the oven and their absence should not deter you from buying the rolls if they look and smell fresh. They are best eaten very fresh, and are noticeably salty, like most Scottish bread. They are popular almost any time of the day, but are a favourite at breakfast, for bacon "butties" and with various fillings. A variation of Scottish "baps" or morning rolls are soft rolls. Confusingly, these rolls are often not as soft as morning rolls. They have a golden glaze, which is produced by brushing the rolls with cream both before and after they are baked.

RIGHT: Morning rolls may be known by different names in Scotland but are all similar, being white, flattish and soft.

IRISH BREADS

WHITE SODA BREAD

Soda bread is the traditional bread of Ireland, which has quite different bread-baking traditions from mainland Britain. The old Irish hearth had no built-in oven, and bread was cooked either on a griddle set over the fire, or in a *bastable*, a type of Dutch oven or oven-pot that would have been set in the smouldering peat. These methods continued to be popular even when iron cooking ranges were introduced to Ireland, and even today specialist Irish bakers will make their traditional breads in cast-iron casseroles with the lid on. Another significant difference in bread making in Ireland was the popularity of bicarbonate of soda, as opposed to yeast, as a raising agent. Buttermilk provides the necessary acid to the alkaline bicarbonate of soda and the best soda breads are made using this, although cream of tartar is often used as an alternative to the buttermilk.

There is a vast range of different soda breads, and almost every bakery in Ireland, as well as most restaurants, has its own favourite recipe. Outside Ireland there is still a reasonable selection of white, brown and wholemeal soda breads available in most supermarkets. Better still are those breads made on the premises by craft bakers. If the baker is Irish, so much the better.

RIGHT: Soda bread can be baked whole and then broken into farls.

Irish round soda bread is normally marked with a cross. Cut the bread into quarters before cooking, and you have soda farls. These are either baked in the oven or cooked on a covered griddle and have a pale, crusty, floury appearance.

OATMEAL SODA BREAD

In a country with a history of more than its fair share of poverty, almost any edible material that could be ground to a meal would have been used for making bread. Oatmeal is high in protein and would have made a nourishing if flattish bread.

BARM BRACK

This is the Irish version of the Welsh bara brith, the words also translating as "speckled bread". It is linked with several Irish festivals, notably St Brighid's Day – 1 February and the first day of spring – and the festival of Luanasa, which celebrated the start of harvest on 1 August. Barm brack is associated with Hallowe'en and there is also a tradition of baking a wedding ring into the bread, the finder being thus assured of becoming engaged before the year is out.

The traditional barm brack, normally made with white flour, is one of the few yeasted Irish breads. Made with sugar, sultanas, mixed peel and currants, it is enriched with butter and eggs. Barm brack is quite delicious by itself, spread with jam or toasted and buttered. It is widely available in Britain and is well worth looking out for.

RIGHT: Barm brack is one of Ireland's most delicious teabreads. Toast and eat with butter or just cut into chunks or serve with jam.

POTATO BREAD

Potatoes, since their introduction in the 17th century, have been an essential food in Ireland. At various times, up to and including the early parts of the 20th century, wheat was scarce and expensive. Potatoes were regularly used to help "stretch" the flour, producing a nourishing and, if lard was available, a well-flavoured griddle bread. Today, potato breads made by blending mashed potatoes with some proportion of white flour are baked by Irish bakers and some restaurants. The dough is then normally marked or cut into farls and either cooked over a griddle or baked in the oven.

RIGHT: This potato bread was formed into a star shape before being baked.

RIGHT: Soda farls are wedges of soda bread, cut from a loaf either before baking or after.

SODA FARLS

As already mentioned in the entry on white soda bread, the term "farl" describes a wedge-shaped soda bread (usually a quarter of a loaf). The word derives from "fardel", which meant "fourth part", and in Ireland, soda bread is often marked into quarters, or "farls", before baking, as indeed is the Yorkshire farl. In addition, some are actually cut into farls (either into quarters or thirds) before baking, to give a thick wedge-shaped bread with a good crust. Most of these soda farls are made using a white flour, although some are wholemeal breads, made with Irish-milled flour and creamy buttermilk. Properly made, soda farls, like soda bread, are delicious. Their main problem is that they stale quickly, so if possible, consume on the day of purchase.

WHEATEN LOAF

This wheaten loaf is a soda bread that is baked in a tin, so that it is "loaf" shaped, rather than the usual rough round. In Ireland, round soda breads are often called "cakes" or "cakes of bread"; whereas a tin-baked soda bread is called a loaf. Wheaten loaves are normally made with soft Irish wholemeal flour.

BELOW: An Irish wheaten loaf, which is a type of soda bread.

IRISH SODA BREAD

225g/8oz/2 cups unbleached
plain flour
225g/8oz/2 cups wholemeal flour, plus
extra for dusting
5ml/1 tsp salt
10ml/2 tsp bicarbonate of soda
10ml/2 tsp cream of tartar
40g/1½ oz/3 tbsp butter or lard
5ml/1 tsp caster sugar
350–375ml/12–13fl oz/1½–1⅔ cups
buttermilk

MAKES 1 ROUND LOAF

VARIATION
Shape into two small loaves and bake
for 25–30 minutes.

*Soda bread can be prepared in minutes and is excellent served warm, fresh
from the oven. You can use all plain white flour, if preferred, to create a bread
with a finer texture.*

1 Preheat the oven to 190°C/375°F/Gas 5.
Lightly grease a baking sheet. Sift the
flour and salt into a large bowl.

2 Add the bicarbonate of soda and
cream of tartar, then rub in the butter or
lard. Stir in the sugar.

3 Pour in sufficient buttermilk to mix to
a soft dough. Do not over-mix or the
bread will be heavy and tough. Shape
into a round on a lightly floured surface.

4 Place on the prepared baking sheet
and mark a cross using a sharp knife,
cutting deep into the dough.

5 Dust lightly with wholemeal flour and
bake for 35–45 minutes or until well
risen and the bread sounds hollow when
tapped on the base. Serve warm.

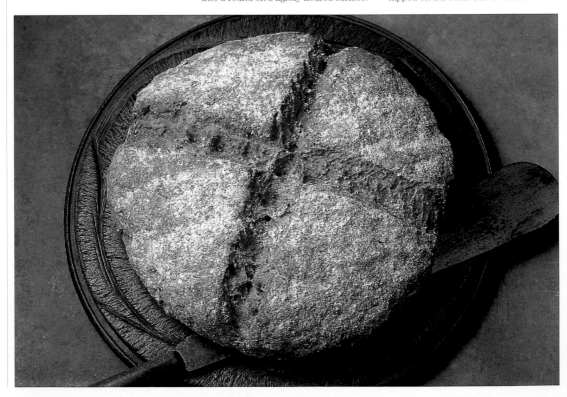

MALTED CURRANT BREAD

This spiced currant bread makes a good tea or breakfast bread, sliced and spread with a generous amount of butter. It also makes superb toast.

50g/2oz/3 tbsp malt extract
30ml/2 tbsp golden syrup
50g/2oz/¼ cup butter
450g/1lb/4 cups unbleached white bread flour
5ml/1 tsp mixed spice
20g/¾ oz fresh yeast
175ml/6fl oz/¾ cup lukewarm milk
175g/6oz/¾ cup currants, slightly warmed

FOR THE GLAZE
30ml/2 tbsp milk
30ml/2 tbsp caster sugar

MAKES 2 LOAVES

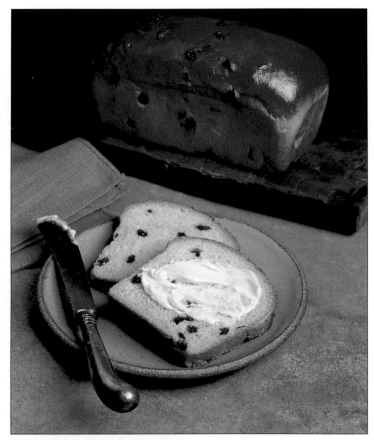

COOK'S TIP
When you are making more than one loaf, the easiest way to prove them is to place the tins in a lightly oiled large polythene bag.

4 Turn the dough out on to a lightly floured surface, knock back, then knead in the currants. Divide the dough in two and shape into two loaves. Place in the prepared tins. Cover with oiled clear film and leave to rise, in a warm place, for 2–3 hours, or until the dough reaches the top of the tins.

5 Meanwhile, preheat the oven to 200°C/400°F/Gas 6. Bake for 35–40 minutes or until golden. While the loaves are baking heat the milk and sugar for the glaze in a small saucepan. Turn out the loaves on to a wire rack, then invert them, so that they are the right way up. Immediately brush the glaze evenly over the loaves and leave to cool.

1 Lightly grease two 450g/1lb loaf tins. Place the malt extract, golden syrup and butter in a saucepan and heat gently until the butter has melted. Set aside to cool completely.

2 Sift the flour and mixed spice together into a large bowl and make a well in the centre. Cream the yeast with a little of the milk, then blend in the remaining milk. Add the yeast mixture and cooled malt mixture to the centre of the flour and blend together to form a dough.

3 Turn out the dough on to a lightly floured surface and knead for about 10 minutes until smooth and elastic. Place in a lightly oiled bowl, cover with lightly oiled clear film and leave to rise, in a warm place, for 1½–2 hours, or until doubled in bulk.

Scottish Morning Rolls

450g/1lb/4 cups unbleached plain white flour, plus extra for dusting
10ml/2 tsp salt
20g/¾ oz fresh yeast
150ml/¼ pint/⅔ cup lukewarm milk
150ml/¼ pint/⅔ cup lukewarm water
30ml/2 tbsp milk, for glazing

MAKES 10 ROLLS

These rolls are best served warm, as soon as they are baked. In Scotland they are a firm favourite for breakfast with a fried egg and bacon.

1 Grease 2 baking sheets. Sift the flour and salt together into a large bowl and make a well in the centre. Mix the yeast with the milk, then mix in the water. Add to the centre of the flour and mix together to form a soft dough.

2 Knead the dough lightly in the bowl, then cover with lightly oiled clear film and leave to rise, in a warm place, for 1 hour, or until doubled in bulk. Turn the dough out on to a lightly floured surface and knock back.

3 Divide the dough into 10 equal pieces. Knead lightly and, using a rolling pin, shape each piece to a flat oval 10 × 7.5cm/4 × 3in or a flat round 9cm/3½ in.

4 Transfer to the prepared baking sheets, spaced well apart, and cover with oiled clear film. Leave to rise, in a warm place, for about 30 minutes.

5 Meanwhile, preheat the oven to 200°C/400°F/Gas 6. Press each roll in the centre with the three middle fingers to equalise the air bubbles and to help prevent blistering. Brush with milk and dust with flour. Bake for 15–20 minutes or until lightly browned. Dust with more flour and cool slightly on a wire rack. Serve warm.

GRANT LOAVES

This quick and easy recipe was created by Doris Grant and was included in her cookbook, published in the 1940s – the dough requires no kneading and takes only a minute to mix. The loaves should keep moist for several days.

1.4kg/3lb/12 cups wholemeal bread flour
15ml/1 tbsp salt
15ml/1 tbsp easy-blend dried yeast
1.2 litres/2 pints/5 cups warm water (35–38°C)
15ml/1 tbsp muscovado sugar

MAKES 3 LOAVES

1 Thoroughly grease 3 loaf tins, each about 21 × 11 × 6cm/8½ × 4½ × 2½ in and set aside in a warm place. Sift the flour and salt together in a large bowl and warm slightly to take off the chill.

2 Sprinkle the dried yeast over 150ml/¼ pint/⅔ cup of the water. After a couple of minutes stir in the sugar. Leave for 10 minutes.

COOK'S TIP
Muscovado sugar gives this bread a rich flavour. An unrefined cane sugar, it is dark and moist.

3 Make a well in the centre of the flour and stir in the yeast mixture and remaining water. The dough should be slippery. Mix for about 1 minute, working the sides into the middle.

4 Divide among the prepared tins, cover with oiled clear film and leave to rise, in a warm place, for 30 minutes, or until the dough has risen by about a third to within 1cm/½ in of the top of the tins.

5 Meanwhile, preheat the oven to 200°C/400°F/Gas 6. Bake for 40 minutes, or until the loaves are crisp and sound hollow when tapped on the base. Turn out on to a wire rack to cool.

FRENCH BREADS

The French are passionate about their bread. A baguette is one of France's most potent symbols and, whether carried in a basket, strapped to a bicycle or simply tucked under a schoolboy's arm on the way to school, it is as much a sign that you are in France as are the streets of Paris or the vineyards of Provence.

Bread is eaten with every meal and with every course apart from dessert. Although, as in most countries, pre-packaged bread is available, the French seem to attach much importance to their bread, and consequently most families eat fresh bread bought daily – if not from their local *boulangerie*, then at least from the fresh bread counter of the supermarket.

By far the majority of loaves consumed in France are baguettes but there are nevertheless many other types of French bread. The *pain de campagne* and the *levains* are popular throughout the country but there are also countless regional breads of all shapes and sizes. Home-made bread is relatively unusual in France, which surely must be because excellent fresh bread is so easily and readily available. Every village has at least one *boulangerie* where bread is made three or four times a day. French people shop daily – sometimes twice daily – for their bread. Baguettes have to be eaten as fresh as possible, and walking or cycling to the bakery is a small price to pay for the treat.

BAGUETTE

The baguette was developed in Paris in the 1930s and came about due to a combination of factors. White bread was becoming increasingly popular, being synonymous, so it was believed at the time, with quality and excellence. The new baker's yeasts that had been developed meant bakers could experiment with other ways of adding yeast to flour, and mechanized kneading and steam ovens led to substantial improvements in techniques and baking. There are many explanations today for why the best baguettes (and they are not all excellent, even in France) are such a delight, yet so difficult to recreate. The soft French flours certainly play a significant part, producing a soft, light crumb with a wonderful wheaty flavour. The small amounts of yeast used, together with a long kneading and rising period and finally, but not least, the skill of the baker, all contribute to the flavour and texture of a baguette, with its sharp, thin crust and delicious, soft crumb.

The baguette was first known as *pain de fantaisie* ("fancy bread") but the word baguette, meaning "stick", was soon adopted, being obviously the more descriptive nomenclature. *Flutes*, *bâtards*, *ficelles*, *pains* and *petits pains* all belong to the same family, made using the same dough and method. *Pain* is a rounder French bread, normally found only in rural areas. The *bâtard* ("bastard") is a cross between the baguette and the *pain*. It is shorter and slightly fatter than a baguette but weighs about the same. The *flute* is a slim 200g/7oz baguette, while the little *ficelle* ("string") is slimmer still, weighing half as much as a baguette. The baguette itself measures some 68cm/27in in length and weighs 250g/9oz. *Petits pains* are individual sized breads and are often eaten for breakfast.

The baguette has been available outside France for some 20 years and thankfully continues to get better and better.

ABOVE: *French baguettes: there are many different varieties, but they should all have a crisp crust and a soft crumb.*

Other baguette-style breads are *baguette à l'ancienne* or *baguette de tradition*, *baguette rustique* and *baguette campagne*, often dark, slightly floury and with small paper labels. These breads are an effort by some traditional bakers to re-create the original baguette, as opposed to the modern version, which has, particularly since the 1970s, been subject to ever-faster production methods. These "traditional" baguettes may be made by a sourdough method, can contain rye or other grains or may be a wholemeal or bran version. You will need to ask to find out.

Although breads sold as French sticks are worth avoiding, more and more baguettes, sold either by French-style bakeries or by discerning supermarkets, can be very good. They are likely to contain the essential soft wheat and may have been imported from France part-baked.

VIENNA ROLLS

These little milk breads and their cousins, *petits pains au lait*, are enriched with milk and egg and are normally served for breakfast. Do not confuse French Vienna rolls with British rolls of the same name, which are a crusty torpedo-shape and made with a plain dough. French

LEFT: Vienna rolls are soft and slightly sweet, making a good choice for breakfast.

Vienna rolls are similar to bridge rolls and are fairly small and soft. They may be slashed three or four times across the top, while *petits pains au lait* are rounded, often with a cross cut on top, or long and tapered at either end. They sometimes have a sprinkling of sugar on top.

BRIOCHE

Brioche is one of France's favourite breakfast breads, made with white flour and yeast, enriched with butter, milk and eggs and sweetened with just a little sugar. It is similar to many of the British enriched breads, such as Sally Lunns, although generally richer, using a half to three-quarters butter to flour ratio, which is as rich as or richer than most pastries. Although not as popular as croissants outside France, brioche makes a perfect bread for breakfast, with its soft texture and rich flavour. It tastes wonderful served with marmalade or a fruit conserve.

Brioche is made in a variety of shapes and sizes. The most

ABOVE: A loaf-shaped brioche and small individual brioche buns.

RIGHT: *The unmistakable crescent-shaped croissant is popular at breakfast almost everywhere.*

famous is undoubtedly the *brioche à tête*, with its fluted sides and little brioche cap perched on top, and which in turn comes in various sizes – from individual buns to large loaves. The *brioche Nanterre* is made by arranging six or eight balls of brioche dough in a zigzag pattern along the bottom of a loaf pan, while the *brioche Parisienne* is made in a similar way, but with nine or ten balls of dough placed in a circle. Both rise to fill out the pan but the divisions still exist so that small chunks can be broken off.

Savoury brioche, made using cheese in place of some of the butter, is becoming more widely available outside France. This is likely to be loaf-shaped, rather than the traditional round, and can be used for savoury dishes (as indeed can the sweeter versions). One of the most delicious ways of using savoury brioche is to hollow out the centre and stuff with wild mushrooms or grilled peppers.

CROISSANTS

Another essentially French creation, these popular pastries are available almost everywhere, served not only for breakfast but stuffed with savoury fillings and sold wherever there is a demand for food that can be eaten on the hoof. In France, a distinction is drawn between the *croissant au beurre*, which is small and straight and is made using butter, and the *croissant ordinaire*, which is the more familiar crescent shape made with vegetable fat. The distinction is by no means clear cut, however, as some producers who use only butter in their croissants favour the crescent shape. If the croissants are prepacked, you can check the packet; otherwise you will need to ask your baker. Ideally, buy croissants fresh in the morning from a local baker, when they will be soft inside, with a slightly crackly crust.

EPI

This translates as "wheat ear" and is the traditional bread at harvest festivals, the French equivalent of a harvest loaf. The little ears of bread are made separately and fashioned into sticks or into a large round called a *couronne* ("crown"). The breads can then be broken off, piece by piece, for eating. *Epis* are normally made using a baguette-style dough and are light and crusty.

FOUGASSE

These large, flat breads are quite unmistakable with their deep cuts representing branches of a tree, cogwheels or even the grate of a fire. They are a speciality of Languedoc and Provence although they originally came from Italy and are closely akin to the Italian focaccia. Sometimes known as *fouacés*, or "hearth bread", they were traditionally baked on the floor of the oven after the embers had been

ABOVE: *Epi is an unusual bread.*

scraped out, but while it was still too hot to bake a normal loaf. There are several varieties of *fougasse* – most use a sour-dough-style leaven and all are flat, deeply cut and baked in a very hot oven.

PAIN DE CAMPAGNE
Next to baguettes, this is the best-known of French breads. In spite of its name, the loaf was the invention of a Parisian baker and is as much enjoyed in towns and cities as it is in the coun-try. Made using a *chef* starter, it has a thick, slightly grey and floury crust and a dis-cernibly sour smell and taste. No rules exist for its shape, although, like almost all French bread, it is oven bottom-baked (i.e. without using tins) and is therefore a convenient round (or a rather misshapen) baton. Outside France and in French cities, the breads are nor-mally of manageable size, weighing about 450g/1lb, but visit a rural *boulangerie* in France and you will find huge cartwheel-size breads or sturdy, long loaves, which will keep a large family going for several days. These are sometimes called *pain ménage* ("household bread") and may be sold by weight. Since it is very

LEFT: Fougasse is the equivalent of Italy's focaccia but has characteristic slashes.

much a local product, you will find the bread changes from region to region, even from village to village. Although most use white wheat flour, rye meal and wholemeal grain is occasionally added, especially for *pain de campagne rustique*, and the flavour and shape will vary enormously. Being a sourdough bread, it keeps well for 4–5 days and indeed is better the day after baking – quite the opposite of the refined baguette.

Pain de campagne is widely available in supermarkets. Shop around for the variety you prefer.

RIGHT: Pain de Campagne comes in many shapes and sizes.

PAIN AUX NOIX

This favourite French bread, although it translates as "nut bread", is understood to be walnut bread. The walnuts give it a teabread feel, but it is very much a savoury bread, best served with soft cheese, such as Brie or Camembert or, if you prefer, strong-flavoured Cheddar or Stilton. It is made using a wholemeal bread flour, which contrasts and complements the nutty and savoury walnuts.

PAIN DE MIE

This is the French version of a British sandwich loaf. It is cooked in an enclosed tin, so that the bread has square sides and a soft crust, making it the ideal shape for sandwiches. Unlike the British loaf, however, it is normally enriched with milk and butter so that, in flavour, it is more like brioche than a plain white loaf.

PAIN DE SEIGLE/PAIN AU SEIGLE

Pain de seigle is French rye and the choice bread for eating with oysters. Regulations insist that it must contain at least two-thirds rye, the remaining proportion made up with wheat flour, which gives it a lighter flavour and colour than German and Scandinavian rye breads. *Pain au seigle* ("bread with rye") needs to contain only some 10 per cent rye and is a lighter bread again.

PAIN POILÂNE

This proprietary loaf is produced and distributed by the famous Poilâne bakers in Paris, not just throughout France, but all

ABOVE: Pain au seigle (left) contains a small amount of rye and has a mild flavour. A brown pain de mie (centre) stands alongside pain aux noix (right), a savoury walnut loaf which is excellent with a strong cheese.

over the world. Based on the traditional and long-forgotten country loaves of France's past, the bakery prides itself on the methods used for making and baking the bread – a natural sourdough leaven is kneaded briefly but long fermented, then hand-moulded and finally baked in wood-fired ovens. Because the sourdough method, by definition, produces a different loaf each time, breads in the shop can vary to a surprising degree, some being wonderful, others disappointing.

PAIN POLKA

A speciality bread of the Loire region, this is an oval or round loaf, somewhat flat and criss-crossed with deep slashes. It is baked using the *levain* method of keeping back part of the previous day's dough and using this as the starter for the bread.

PAIN BATTU AU FROMAGE

This is a cheese batter bread, which uses Parmesan cheese, a fact that suggests that the bread originally came from Italy or the Alpes-Maritimes region of France. The cheese is stirred into the batter and also sprinkled over the top before baking, to give a golden crust. The bread can be loaf-shaped or baked in brioche-style individual tins.

PAIN ALLEMAND AUX FRUITS

This translates as German fruit bread, but is nevertheless a French bread from Strasbourg, a city on the border with Germany. Strasbourg is in the heart of Alsace, a region famous for its rich breads, notably *kugelhopf*.
Pain Allemand is a rich fruit bread

ABOVE: Pain polka can be plain or may contain chopped olives.

LEFT: Pain poilâne is easily recognized by the four slashes making a rough square on its top.

ABOVE: There are many variations on pain au levain (back) but all will be made using the sourdough method. The boule de meule is a very substantial loaf best eaten with hearty soups and stews.

that is spiced with cinnamon, cloves and aniseed and rich with raisins, prunes, apricots and figs. It is, needless to say, a festive bread.

PAIN AU LEVAIN

A white or sometimes wholemeal bread that has become almost as popular in the United Kingdom as it is in France. A *levain* is a bread made by the natural sour-dough method, *levain* being the French expression for a sourdough. The breads come in a variety of shapes, often resembling a rather short and flat baguette, or can be moulded into rough squares. *Pain rustique* is made using the same sour-dough method, but using a proportion of wholemeal flour or a blend of grains.

BOULE DE MEULE

The word *boulangerie* comes from the French word for a round of dough, *une boule*, which also accounts for the name of this bread. *Boule de meule* translates literally as a round of stoneground dough, which pretty well sums up this bread, except that it is baked, ideally on the sole of the oven, until it is crusty. *Boules de meule* are normally quite large, with an excellent flavour.

GÂTEAU DE GANNAT

This rich festive bread is popular in the Gannatois region of France. Its principal distinguishing feature is the fromage blanc which is stirred into the batter-like dough with eggs and butter to make a soft crumbly loaf with a sweet/sour flavour. This taste is particularly noticeable if brandy has been added.

PAIN DE PROVENCE

Provence is so rich in all sorts of wonder-ful foods that it would be nonsense to

RIGHT: Cereale is normally a torpedo-shaped loaf.

ascribe a single bread to this region. If you visit Provence you are likely to find a range of *pains de Provence*, either fashioned roughly into small loaves or made into slender baguettes. Along with the herbs of Provence – savory, thyme and basil – the dough is made with lavender flowers and fennel. It has a heady flavour and is superb served with cheese or to accompany a soup.

CEREALE

This is a well-flavoured light brown loaf with a good crust and a tender crumb. It is made from eight cereals and seeds and typically includes wheat, corn, rye, millet, malted wheat and oats, with sunflower and sesame seeds. The shape is quite distinctive. *Cereale* is usually formed into a broad torpedo shape and is lightly dusted with flour.

BELGIAN BREADS

PISTOLET

Pistolets are the Belgian equivalent to the croissants of France. They are small, butter-enriched round rolls, easily distinguished by their central indentation, which is made using a stick dipped in oil before baking. They have a soft texture under a thin, glossy crust and can be found in many parts of northern France, too, where they are just as popular as they are in their native Belgium. *Pistolets* are normally enjoyed for breakfast or for tea, split and spread with preserve or, alternatively, are broken into chunks and eaten French-style dipped in café au lait.

CRAMIQUE

A popular Belgian teabread, this is stuffed with raisins and enriched with butter and milk. It is rather squat in shape and can be made using a wholemeal or a white flour, or a blend of the two. Whiter versions have a soft crumb with the texture and flavour of brioche, while the wholemeal *cramique* has a more malted flavour. Bought fresh, *cramique* is wonderful simply buttered or spread with a preserve. Breads that are two or three days old taste good toasted, buttered and spread with jam, or served with a soft cheese, such as Brie or Camembert.

ABOVE: Fruity cramique

FOUGASSE

A fougasse is a lattice-shaped, flattish loaf from the South of France. It can be cooked as a plain bread or flavoured with cheese, anchovies, herbs, nuts or olives. On Christmas Eve in Provence a fougasse flavoured with orange flower water is part of a table centrepiece of thirteen desserts, used to symbolize Christ and the Twelve Apostles.

450g/1lb/4 cups unbleached white bread flour
5ml/1 tsp salt
20g/³/4 oz fresh yeast
280ml/9fl oz/generous 1 cup lukewarm water
15ml/1 tbsp extra virgin olive oil

FOR THE FILLING
50g/2oz/¹/3 cup Roquefort cheese, crumbled
40g/1¹/2oz/¹/3 cup walnut pieces, chopped
25g/1oz/2 tbsp drained, canned anchovy fillets, soaked in milk and drained again, chopped
olive oil, for brushing

MAKES 2 LOAVES

VARIATIONS
• Replace the cheese with 15ml/1 tbsp chopped fresh sage or thyme or 40g/1½oz/⅓ cup chopped pitted olives.
• To make a sweet fougasse, replace 15ml/1 tbsp of the water with orange flower water. Include 50g/2oz/⅓ cup chopped candied orange peel and 25g/1oz/2 tbsp sugar.

2 Place the dough in a lightly oiled bowl, cover with lightly oiled clear film and leave to rise, in a warm place, for about 1 hour, or until doubled in bulk.

3 Turn out on to a lightly floured surface and knock back the dough. Divide into 2 equal pieces and flatten one piece of dough. Sprinkle over the cheese and walnuts and fold the dough over on itself 2–3 times to incorporate. Repeat with the remaining piece of dough, this time incorporating the anchovies. Shape each piece of flavoured dough into a ball.

4 Flatten each ball of dough and fold the bottom third up and the top third down, to make an oblong. Roll the cheese dough into a rectangle measuring about 28 × 15cm/11 × 6in. Using a sharp knife, make 4 diagonal cuts almost to the edge. Pull and stretch the dough evenly, so that it resembles a ladder.

5 Shape the anchovy dough into an oval with a flat base, about 25cm/10in long. Using a sharp knife, make 3 diagonal slits on each side towards the flat base, and pull to open the cuts. Transfer to the prepared baking sheets, cover with lightly oiled clear film and leave to rise, in a warm place, for about 30–45 minutes, or until nearly doubled in bulk.

6 Meanwhile, preheat the oven to 220°C/425°F/Gas 7. Brush both loaves with a little olive oil and bake for 25 minutes, or until golden. Transfer to a wire rack to cool.

1 Lightly grease 2 baking sheets. Sift the flour and salt together into a large bowl and make a well in the centre. In a measuring jug, cream the yeast with 60ml/4 tbsp of the water. Pour the yeast mixture into the centre of the flour with the remaining water and the olive oil and mix to a soft dough. Turn out on to a lightly floured surface and knead the dough for 8–10 minutes until smooth and elastic.

PAIN AUX NOIX

This delicious butter- and milk-enriched wholemeal bread is filled with walnuts. It is the perfect companion for cheese.

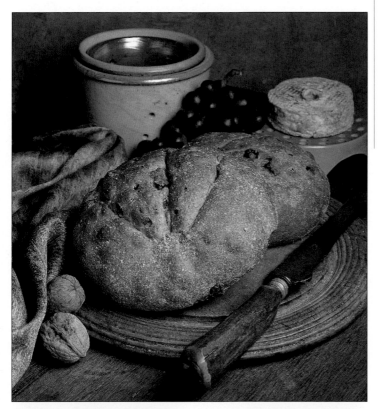

*50g/2oz/1/4 cup butter
350g/12oz/3 cups wholemeal
bread flour
115g/4oz/1 cup unbleached white
bread flour
15ml/1 tbsp light brown
muscovado sugar
7.5ml/1 1/2 tsp salt
20g/3/4 oz fresh yeast
275ml/9fl oz/generous 1 cup
lukewarm milk
175g/6oz/1 1/2 cups walnut pieces*

MAKES 2 LOAVES

3 Knead on a lightly floured surface for 6–8 minutes. Place in a lightly oiled bowl, cover with lightly oiled clear film and leave to rise, in a warm place, for 1 hour, or until doubled in bulk.

4 Turn out the dough on to a lightly floured surface and gently knock back. Press or roll out to flatten and then sprinkle over the nuts. Gently press the nuts into the dough, then roll it up. Return to the oiled bowl, re-cover and leave, in a warm place, for 30 minutes.

5 Turn out on to a lightly floured surface, divide in half and shape each piece into a ball. Place on the baking sheets, cover with lightly oiled clear film and leave to rise, in a warm place, for 45 minutes, or until doubled in bulk.

6 Meanwhile, preheat the oven to 220°C/425°F/Gas 7. Using a sharp knife, slash the top of each loaf 3 times. Bake for about 35 minutes, or until the loaves sound hollow when tapped on the base. Transfer to a wire rack to cool.

1 Lightly grease 2 baking sheets. Place the butter in a small saucepan and heat until melted and starting to turn brown, then set aside to cool. Mix the flours, sugar and salt in a large bowl and make a well in the centre. Cream the yeast with half the milk. Add to the centre of the flour with the remaining milk.

2 Pour the cool melted butter through a fine strainer into the centre of the flour so that it joins the liquids already there. Using your hand, mix the liquids together in the bowl and gradually mix in small quantities of the flour to make a batter. Continue until the mixture forms a moist dough.

ITALIAN BREADS

Italian bread has had something of a renaissance in the past few years and rightly so. Italian breads are a delight, delicious served with pasta, fish, meats and poultry, as well as cheese. Any Italian baker will tell you that there are thousands of different Italian breads. This could actually be true should anyone ever try to count! Italy was once made up of a number of independent states, and each developed its own favourite cuisine, including, of course, breads. Geography and climate played a part, as did prosperity. Some of the best-known loaves, such as ciabatta and *pagnotta* are "national" breads, available everywhere. Other breads – the more peasant-style loaves – from rural areas would have been coarse, mealy loaves, made with whatever grain could be gathered together. Olive oil was frequently added, not only for flavour, but to add extra nourishment and to help the keeping qualities of the loaf. Nowadays these rustic loaves are still made using olive oil. They are normally white, although wholemeal and mixed grain loaves are not unheard of. They can be yeast-leavened but originally would have been made using a natural leaven. Small bakeries, especially those in the south of Italy, a region only mildly influenced by tourism and fashion, still produce these loaves for their loyal customers, made in the traditional way from time-honoured recipes. If you visit these parts, be sure to buy and sample some of these regional breads; you cannot fail to be delighted. Outside Italy, various country-style breads, such as *pagnotta* and *pugliese*, are available from Italian-style bakers, although these loaves are likely to be standardized. Nevertheless, many first-generation Italian bakers in Britain and North America, who learnt their baking skills from their parents and grandparents, bake their own favourite regional bread and these are likely to be as good and authentic as the breads of their homeland.

The distinguishing feature of most Italian breads, especially those bought from an Italian-style baker, is the shape rather than the dough. By and large, bakers do not make up different doughs for different breads – they would not have the time, the space or the labour. The difference lies in the shaping, the slashing and the baking – a small distinction you may think, but wait until you try the bread and you will be surprised.

BIOVA

This regional bread comes from the north of Italy, around Piedmont. It is cylindrical in shape with little pointed horns. Made with lard, it has a thick crust and soft crumb and has an excellent flavour.

CARTA DA MUSICA

This extraordinary harvest sheaf loaf from Sardinia, also sometimes called *carasaù*, is made with paper thin leaves of dough, piled up to make a tower that looks like a stack of uneven shaped pancakes. The leaves of bread are brittle but can be eaten as a snack with an aperitif or with salads. Alternatively, the leaves of bread can be softened in a light dressing or even just water and olive oil, then wrapped around a filling.

CIABATTA

This ubiquitous loaf has surprisingly not suffered for all that it is produced on a massive scale so as to be available from almost every supermarket in the country.

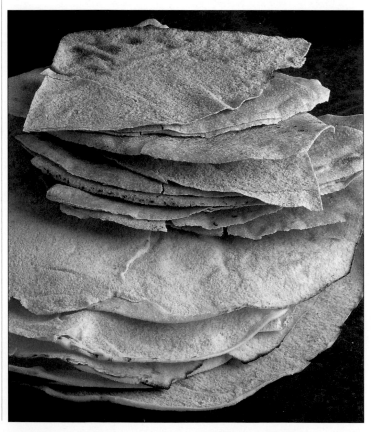

LEFT: Carta da musica means sheets of music and does look not unlike sheets of parchment piled on top of each other.

LEFT: Plain ciabatta served with olive and sun-dried tomato versions.

It is an oval, slightly flattish loaf, and looks rather like a squashed slipper, which is what the word, rather unromantically, means. It is made with generous quantities of olive oil and has a thin, friable crust. The crumb is light, holey and slightly chewy. Ciabatta is delicious served as an accompaniment to soups or tomato salads, as it will mop up the juices beautifully.

Like the French baguette, ciabatta is a relatively new shape of bread. It is normally a white loaf, made using a sponge dough method – flour, yeast and water are fermented for up to 24 hours before being incorporated into the rest of the dough. Another particular feature of ciabatta, making it a tricky bread to bake at home, is the soft consistency of the dough. It has a minimum of 75 per cent water and oil and is thus quite unlike any other kind of bread. A long kneading process also contributes to ciabatta's unique flavour, which should be sweet/sour, as well as its texture: a crisp crust and an open crumb. Numerous flavourings can be added to ciabatta – from olives and sun-dried tomatoes to cheese and walnuts. Many supermarket loaves are sold part-baked and should be finished off in a hot oven before being served. The final baking enhances both the flavour and texture of what is undeniably one of the world's favourite breads.

FOCACCIA AND FOCACCETTE

Focaccia is another Italian bread that has captured the imagination of the rest of the world. Known variously as "Italian country flat bread", *pizza rustica* or *pizza genovese*, it is a large, flat bread, slightly puffy when fresh and dimpled all over the surface with little indentations. It can be round, square or a rather misshapen rectangle; shape is not particularly important. This is the original Italian hearth bread, made from surplus pieces of dough and baked at a very high heat before the oven cooled slightly for the massive family loaves. It is easy to imagine the children waiting impatiently for their share of the warm bread as it came out of the oven. Today, most shop-bought focaccia, particularly those from supermarkets, are round and can be rather bland in flavour. However, Italian bakers who know and love this bread will produce far more tasty loaves, baking them in a very hot oven so that, like pizzas, they are floury and flecked with black.

Focaccia is a wonderfully versatile bread. Apart from the olive oil that is kneaded into the basic dough, the flattish bread can be sprinkled with sea salt, herbs,

BELOW: Focaccia is often sprinkled with crushed rosemary.

onions, prosciutto or cheese. Smaller versions of focaccia, *focaccette*, are small rolls sprinkled with salt and onions.

GRISSINI

These long, thin breadsticks, mainly popular as an aperitif, are made from wheat flour and have been cooked until completely dry, so that they are basically all crust and no crumb. The better grissini are made using olive oil; best of all are those that are hand-made by craft bakers, having considerably more character than the bland, smooth breadsticks available in most supermarkets.

Grissini come from the north-west of Italy, around Turin and Piedmont. Here they also make a more substantial type of breadstick, called *francescine*. These are thicker breadsticks with a softer centre and they not only have a better flavour, but have a decidedly good crunch, too. Grissini are mostly made using white flour, although wholemeal ones are sometimes available, especially if made on the

BELOW: Paesana

ABOVE: The best grissini are bought from Italian bakers or delicatessens.

premises by smaller bakers. Grissini are commonly rolled in poppy seeds or sesame seeds or coarsely ground sea salt before baking to add extra flavour.

MICHETTA

This is a round white roll with a well-flavoured crust, which is called *rosetta* in Rome.

MEZZA LUNA

This simple crusty loaf is shaped like a half moon. It is made with the standard white dough used for *pagnotta* and other country breads.

PAESANA

This round, simple white loaf that is cross-cut to divide into farls, tastes rather like focaccia or ciabatta. *Paesana* is generally less rich in olive oil and, without the addition of herbs, sun-dried tomatoes or olives, tends be a far plainer loaf than its cousins. It is never-theless very good with soups and stews.

PAGNOTTA

This large, round farmhouse loaf is prob-ably the most common and popular bread in Italy, sold all over the country. Loaves can be small and round, but in Italy some may be huge, cut in portions, each still big enough to feed a large family. The bread is traditionally made using the sourdough method. Outside the country, some Italian delicatessens sell this bread, either imported from Italy or made to an origi-nal recipe. Italian-style bakers, however, do not always use the classic but lengthy process for their breads. They argue that for most, *pagnotta* means a standard wheat loaf, so they use the same dough as for other Italian breads. In Italy *pagnotta* can be white, wholemeal or a mixture, depending on the region, and all types are available outside Italy, with white being the most common.

PANE AL CIOCCOLATO

A yeasted bread made with olive oil and studded with dark chocolate which is kneaded into the dough, it can be whole-meal, but is more commonly coloured a rich brown with cocoa powder. In Italy, chocolate bread is served with mas-carpone or Gorgonzola cheese as a snack.

PANE CON NOCI

There are several different Italian breads

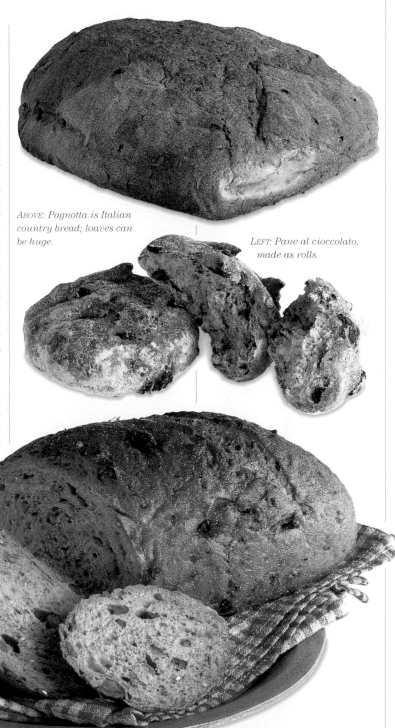

ABOVE: Pagnotta is Italian country bread; loaves can be huge.

LEFT: Pane al cioccolato, made as rolls.

RIGHT: Pane con noci is a savoury nut bread.

that go under the title of "bread with nuts". The oval-shaped bread is similar to the British and French walnut breads, while a slim, flat loaf with sultanas and walnuts is a sweet version of ciabatta.

PANETTONE

Panettone is a Milanese speciality, sold around Christmas as a traditional festive cake. In Italy and in delicatessens outside the country, it is sold wrapped in cellophane and tied with coloured ribbons. For all its richness – made with liberal amounts of butter, eggs and milk, together with sultanas, candied peel and sometimes chocolate – *panettone* is surprisingly light in texture. This may have something to do with the traditional *panettone* shape, which is like a squat cylinder or dome, slightly wider at the top where the bread has billowed out into a deep golden crust.

PANE DI MAIS

Made using polenta, a coarse ground cornmeal, *pane di*

RIGHT:
Panettone is the classic Christmas bread.

RIGHT: Pugliese is one of the best-known and loved Italian breads.

mais is one of the few Italian corn breads. It normally also contains some olive oil. It is flatter than most Italian breads, owing to the high proportion of corn, but pieces are perfect for mopping up sauces and salad dressings.

PANE TOSCANO (TUSCAN SALTLESS BREAD)

Alternatively called *pane sciocco* or *pane sciapo Toscano*, this bread is a favourite among Tuscans, who love it for the flavour of the wheat, which is more pronounced in the absence of salt. The bread was made at a time when salt was heavily taxed. Unlike many Italian breads, *pane sciocco* does not contain olive oil either. If you try eating it by itself, a common reaction is "something's wrong", or "something's missing from this bread". However, eaten with goat's cheese, anchovies, olives or salami, the bread comes into its own.

PUGLIESE

This much-loved Italian bread was once the regional bread from Puglia, in the southern region of Apulia. Perhaps it is the extra virgin olive oil from this region or the excellence of the wheat, but *pugliese*

RIGHT: Sfilatino look like small baguettes.

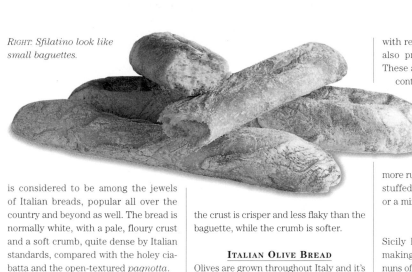

is considered to be among the jewels of Italian breads, popular all over the country and beyond as well. The bread is normally white, with a pale, floury crust and a soft crumb, quite dense by Italian standards, compared with the holey ciabatta and the open-textured *pagnotta*.

SFILATINO

Looking something like a French baguette that has perhaps been crossed with a baby ciabatta, these little Italian breads are a wonderful addition to the bread counter at the supermarket and are excellent served with an Italian meal. Although similar in shape to the baguette, any comparison ends there. *Sfilatino* loaves are noticeably smaller than the baguette, without the slashes on top and with a darker, more floury crust. Made using lots of virgin olive oil,

the crust is crisper and less flaky than the baguette, while the crumb is softer.

ITALIAN OLIVE BREAD

Olives are grown throughout Italy and it's not surprising to find all sorts of olive bread. The more commercially produced loaves are enriched with eggs and butter and normally contain pitted green olives and sometimes whole olives stuffed, Spanish-style,

with red pimiento. Smaller bakers often also produce their own olive breads. These are plainer doughs, which usually contain black olives, sometimes pitted, but sometimes not – so take care when biting into a slice.

TORTINO

Tortino is similar to an olive bread, but is much larger and more rustic, with a dense crumb. It can be stuffed with olives, spinach or tomatoes or a mixture of all these.

SICILIAN SCROLL

Sicily has a strong tradition of bread making. Over the centuries, monks and nuns of the island's many monasteries perfected their baking skills as a sign of devotion to God. Sicilian scroll is unusual in that it contains a high proportion of semolina. Shaped into a broad "S", it has a soft, pale yellow crumb and a crisp crust that is traditionally topped with sesame seeds.

ABOVE:
Pane Toscano goes by several names, including "sciocco" and "Tuscan saltless bread". It has a dense crumb, which to palates unused to its salt-free nature is very bland. However, it has its devotees and is good with cheese.

POLENTA BREAD

Polenta is widely used in Italian cooking. Here it is combined with pine nuts to make a truly Italian bread with a fantastic flavour.

50g/2oz/1/2 cup polenta
300ml/1/2 pint/11/4 cups lukewarm
water
15g/1/2 oz fresh yeast
2.5ml/1/2 tsp clear honey
225g/8oz/2 cups unbleached white
bread flour
25g/1oz/2 tbsp butter
45ml/3 tbsp pine nuts
7.5ml/11/2 tsp salt

FOR THE TOPPING
1 egg yolk
15ml/1 tbsp water
pine nuts, for sprinkling

MAKES 1 LOAF

1 Lightly grease a baking sheet. Mix the polenta and 250ml/8fl oz/1 cup of the water together in a saucepan and slowly bring to the boil, stirring continuously with a large wooden spoon. Reduce the heat and simmer for 2–3 minutes, stirring occasionally. Set aside to cool for 10 minutes, or until just warm.

2 In a small bowl, mix the yeast with the remaining water and honey until creamy. Sift 115g/4oz/1 cup of the flour into a large bowl. Gradually beat in the yeast mixture, then gradually stir in the polenta mixture to combine. Turn out on to a lightly floured surface and knead for 5 minutes until smooth and elastic.

3 Cover the bowl with lightly oiled clear film or a lightly oiled polythene bag. Leave the dough to rise, in a warm place, for about 2 hours, or until it has doubled in bulk.

4 Meanwhile, melt the butter in a small pan, add the pine nuts and cook over a medium heat, stirring, until pale golden. Set aside to cool.

5 Add the remaining flour and the salt to the polenta dough and mix to a soft dough. Knead in the pine nuts. Turn out on to a lightly floured surface and knead for 5 minutes until smooth and elastic.

6 Place in a lightly oiled bowl, cover with lightly oiled clear film and leave to rise, in a warm place, for 1 hour, or until doubled in bulk.

7 Knock back the dough and turn it out on to a lightly floured surface. Cut the dough into 2 equal pieces and roll each piece into a fat sausage about 38cm/15in long. Plait together and place on the prepared baking sheet. Cover with lightly oiled clear film and leave to rise, in a warm place, for 45 minutes. Meanwhile, preheat the oven to 200°C/400°F/Gas 6.

8 Mix the egg yolk and water and brush over the loaf. Sprinkle with pine nuts and bake for 30 minutes, or until golden and sounding hollow when tapped on the base. Cool on a wire rack.

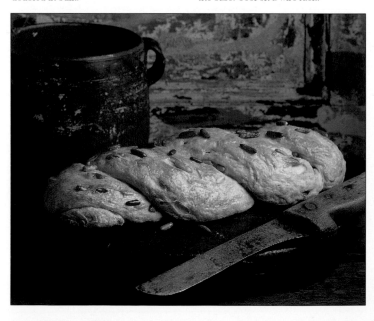

PANE TOSCANO

This bread from Tuscany is made without salt and probably originates from the days when salt was heavily taxed. To compensate for the lack of salt, this bread is usually served with salty foods, such as anchovies and olives.

550g/1¼ lb/5 cups unbleached white bread flour
350ml/12fl oz/1½ cups boiling water
15g/½ oz fresh yeast
60ml/4 tbsp lukewarm water

MAKES 1 LOAF

COOK'S TIP
Salt controls the action of yeast in bread so the leavening action is more noticeable. Don't let this unsalted bread over-rise or it may collapse.

6 Fold the sides of the round into the centre and seal. Place seam side up on the prepared baking sheet. Cover with lightly oiled clear film and leave to rise, in a warm place, for 30–45 minutes, or until doubled in size.

7 Flatten the loaf to about half its risen height and flip over. Cover with a large upturned bowl and leave to rise, in a warm place, for 30 minutes.

1 First make the starter. Sift 175g/6oz/ 1½ cups of the flour into a large bowl. Pour over the boiling water, leave for a couple of minutes, then mix well. Cover the bowl with a damp dish towel and leave for 10 hours.

2 Lightly flour a baking sheet. Cream the yeast with the lukewarm water. Stir into the starter.

3 Gradually add the remaining flour and mix to form a dough. Turn out on to a lightly floured surface and knead for 5–8 minutes until smooth and elastic.

4 Place in a lightly oiled bowl, cover with lightly oiled clear film and leave to rise, in a warm place, for 1–1½ hours, or until doubled in bulk.

5 Turn out the dough on to a lightly floured surface, knock back, and shape into a round.

8 Meanwhile, preheat the oven to 220°C/ 425°F/Gas 7. Slash the top of the loaf, using a sharp knife, if wished. Bake for 30–35 minutes, or until golden. Transfer to a wire rack to cool.

SICILIAN SCROLL

A wonderful pale yellow, crusty-topped loaf, enhanced with a nutty flavour from the sesame seeds. It's perfect for serving with cheese.

450g/1lb/4 cups finely ground semolina
115g/4oz/1 cup unbleached white bread flour
10ml/2 tsp salt
20g/3/4 oz fresh yeast
360ml/12 1/2 fl oz/generous 1 1/2 cups lukewarm water
30ml/2 tbsp extra virgin olive oil
sesame seeds, for sprinkling

MAKES 1 LOAF

4 Turn out on to a lightly floured surface and knock back. Knead gently, then shape into a fat roll about 50cm/20in long. Form into an "S" shape.

5 Carefully transfer the dough to the prepared baking sheet, cover with lightly oiled clear film and leave to rise, in a warm place, for 30–45 minutes, or until doubled in size.

6 Meanwhile, preheat the oven to 220°C/425°F/Gas 7. Brush the top of the scroll with water and sprinkle with sesame seeds. Bake for 10 minutes. Spray the inside of the oven with water twice during this time. Reduce the oven temperature to 200°C/400°F/Gas 6 and bake for a further 25–30 minutes, or until golden. Transfer to a wire rack to cool.

1 Lightly grease a baking sheet. Mix the semolina, white bread flour and salt together in a large bowl and make a well in the centre.

2 In a jug, cream the yeast with half the water, then stir in the remainder. Add the creamed yeast to the centre of the semolina mixture with the olive oil and gradually incorporate the semolina and flour to form a firm dough.

3 Turn out the dough on to a lightly floured surface and knead for 8–10 minutes until smooth and elastic. Place in a lightly oiled bowl, cover with lightly oiled clear film and leave to rise, in a warm place, for 1–1 1/2 hours, or until doubled in bulk.

VARIATION
Although sesame seeds are the traditional topping on this delectable Italian bread, poppy seeds, or even crystals of sea salt, could be used instead.

OLIVE BREAD

Black and green olives and good-quality fruity olive oil combine to make this strongly flavoured and irresistible Italian bread.

1 Lightly grease a baking sheet. Mix the flours, yeast and salt together in a large bowl and make a well in the centre.

2 Add the water and oil to the centre of the flour and mix to a soft dough. Knead the dough on a lightly floured surface for 8–10 minutes until smooth and elastic. Place in a lightly oiled bowl, cover with lightly oiled clear film and leave to rise, in a warm place, for 1 hour, or until doubled in bulk.

3 Turn out on to a lightly floured surface and knock back. Flatten out and sprinkle over the olives. Fold up and knead to distribute the olives. Leave to rest for 5 minutes, then shape into an oval loaf. Place on the prepared baking sheet.

4 Make 6 deep cuts in the top of the loaf, and gently push the sections over. Cover with lightly oiled clear film and leave to rise, in a warm place, for 30–45 minutes, or until doubled in size.

275g/10oz/2¹/₂ cups unbleached white bread flour
50g/2oz/¹/₂ cup wholemeal bread flour
6g/¹/₄ oz sachet easy-blend dried yeast
2.5ml/¹/₂ tsp salt
210ml/7¹/₂ fl oz/scant 1 cup lukewarm water
15ml/1 tbsp extra virgin olive oil, plus extra, for brushing
115g/4oz/1 cup pitted black and green olives, coarsely chopped

MAKES 1 LOAF

VARIATIONS
• Increase the proportion of wholemeal flour to make the loaf more rustic.
• Add some hazelnuts or pine nuts.

5 Meanwhile, preheat the oven to 200°C/400°F/Gas 6. Brush the bread with olive oil and bake for 35 minutes. Transfer to a wire rack to cool.

SPANISH BREADS

Bread is the symbol of all food in Spain. In villages, where bread is still often made at home, the housewife will kiss and make the sign of the Cross over the loaf before baking, and children are taught never to snatch bread as this is seen as a sign of disrespect, not only to their parents but also to God.

If you visit Spain, you are likely to find that the first breads of the day are the morning rolls, such as *bollo* or *chica* (meaning "little girl"). Later in the morning the *panadería* (bakery) will start producing larger breads. These are of almost every conceivable shape and size, but will mostly be yeast-fermented, white, wheat breads. Spain is famous for its simple white breads, with their smooth crust and soft white crumb. Bread is eaten with every meal and with every course. More simple still, and a tradition much loved by the Spanish, is the custom of pouring virgin olive oil over fresh bread to eat as a snack at any time of the day.

While wheat is the principal crop, oats, barley and other cereals are sometimes blended with wheat flour for more rustic loaves. In the north-west corner of the country, in Santiago and La Coruña, wholemeal and rye breads can be found. Here, near the north of Portugal, cornmeal is blended with wheat flour to make rich yellow loaves. Corn was brought back to Spain from the New World by sailors returning home, but is not as popular today in Spain as it is in Portugal.

PAN CATETO

This is the traditional Spanish country bread, made from a starter called the *levadura de masa*.

BELOW: The pan gallego often looks like a squashy cottage loaf with a top knot.

HORNAZO

This is a Castilian flat bread customarily made at Easter. The dough is filled with chunks of *chorizo* (spicy sausage), cheese and hard-boiled eggs so that when it is baked and cut, everybody receives a different piece of bread. *Horno* is the Spanish word for an oven, from which the bread probably gets its name. At one time in Spain, people would take loaves of bread, as well as large joints of meat, turkeys or even whole lambs, to the local baker's for cooking in the stone *horno*.

PAN GALLEGO

This country-style bread is made using olive oil and has a pleasant, unassuming flavour. It can be a rather misshapen round, and a whole loaf can be huge. Much of the *pan gallego* sold outside Spain are quarters of a large loaf. The crust is soft and floury, the crumb light with an open texture. Seed *gallego* is a similar loaf but is studded with pumpkin and sesame seeds, which give it a delicious flavour and texture.

BELOW: Pan aceite

PAN QUEMADO

This is one of the best-known of Spanish sweet breads. It has a rather squashed, sunken look, a bit like an enlarged English lardy cake with its glossy brown top, but in spite of appearances, this is a delicious sweet loaf, a little like a French brioche in texture, although it is made with olive oil rather than butter.

GOFIO

This unusual bread is classified as Spanish, coming as it does from the Canary Islands, but has a fascinating and ancient history that suggests it might more rightly belong with the Arabian or Moroccan breads. Although the Canaries have belonged to Spain for hundreds of years, they were once the home of a group of Berbers called the Guanches. Now extinct, little knowledge of these original people remains apart from a few artefacts. *Gofio*, however, is thought to be a survival of these North African people. The bread is the shape of a large ball and is made from a variety of flours – wheat, barley, corn and gram (dried chick-peas), which are sometimes blended and always toasted before milling. The dough is mixed with water or milk and, although yeast is used today, originally the dough would have been fermented using a natural leaven. Once risen, the bread is baked, either conventionally in an oven or, even today in some parts of the Canaries, in a Dutch oven, a pot-like construction where the embers of the fire are piled around the outside of the pot. The result is a crusty round loaf with a fairly dense crumb, quite unlike the light and airy Spanish breads, and indeed unlike most traditional Moroccan breads as well, which are mostly flat and baked very quickly in unusually hot ovens. Perhaps the scarcity of wheat meant these ancient people needed to be more inventive, or perhaps their settled life on the islands, as opposed to the nomadic life of the Berbers, meant they had more time for the task of baking.

ENSAIMADAS

A speciality of Majorca (Mallorca), these small yeasted pastry buns are the Spanish answer to the croissant, except that instead of being crescent-shaped they look more like little Moorish turbans. Normally a little sweeter than croissants, they have the same soft texture and are served at breakfast with jam or honey in the island's many hotels. Consignments of these little rolls are regularly sent to Barcelona, where they are much appreciated by both tourists and local city dwellers.

A much larger version of the *ensaimada* can also be found in Majorca. This is often topped with cream or a sweet custard-like topping made with pumpkin pulp, sugar, lemon juice and spices. This dessert is particularly popular at fiestas, when the *ensaimada* is decorated with small pieces of marrow and thin slices of *sobrasada*, a type of Majorcan sausage.

MAJORCAN POTATO BUNS

Although a relatively small group of islands, the Balearic Islands have a surprisingly rich and varied cuisine. Along with their own local fish and meat dishes, they have a variety of delicious breads, including these Majorcan potato buns. These small buns are made using either sweet or ordinary potatoes. They have a very sweet taste and are normally eaten at breakfast, during mid-morning or for tea, and are usually served with jam or honey.

PAN ACEITE (OLIVE OIL BREAD)

This is similar to the French *fougasse* and the Italian *foccacia* breads. *Pan Aceite* is commonly a rather misshapen-looking bread. It is baked on the sole of the oven, after being brushed liberally with olive oil (hence the name olive oil bread).

TWELFTH NIGHT BREAD

In Spain and Portugal children receive their presents not on Christmas Day but on Twelfth Night (5 January). Appropriately for the Epiphany, the gifts are delivered by a figure representing the Magi, the three wise men who made their journey from the East to bring gifts to the infant Jesus. It is customary for a special bread called *roscon de reyes* in Spain and *bolo-rei* in Portugal to be baked for this day. The rich teabread is stuffed with fruits and candied peel and traditionally contains a coin or figurine, bringing luck to the person who is given the piece of bread in which it is discovered.

PORTUGUESE BREADS

Portuguese bakers, like their counterparts in other countries, frequently use the same basic dough for making loaves and rolls. It is the shape and manner of baking that gives each bread its own idiosyncratic flavour and texture. Many Portuguese breads are made using a yeasted white flour dough.

ALENTEJANO

This is a white bread with a fairly thick crust and a well-flavoured crumb, which has a distinctive, salty/sour flavour. Like almost all Portuguese and Spanish breads, the bread is oven bottom-baked and has an even, golden crust.

BROA DE MILO

This simple loaf from Minho in northern Portugal, the name of which translates as "corn bread", is normally referred to simply as *broa* and is eaten by everyone. Corn is a popular grain for making bread in Portugal and Spain. The conquistadors and sailors brought home not only potatoes, tomatoes and peppers, but corn as

RIGHT: Alentejano has a good flavour.

BELOW: Papo secos are soft yet crusty.

ABOVE: Rosquilha is an attractive round bread.

well, together with the skills needed to grind it into meal. Corn proved to be a successful crop in the north of Portugal where wheat does not flourish, and it would have been quickly selected as the preferred crop. It is likely that even from the beginning, bakers would have blended cornmeal with wheat in order to provide some gluten, but when this was scarce barley and alfalfa flour was used and, even today, loaves are made from a mixed grain. *Broa de milo* is a robust, well-flavoured loaf, which goes well with Portuguese soups and *cozidos* – stewed meat, vegetables and pulses.

ROSQUILHA

This is a ring-shaped white bread with a pleasant crust and a slightly chewy texture and salty flavour. It will normally be made using the same dough as *alentejano* but the shape means *rosquilha* is crustier, although it does not stay fresh as long. *Rosquilha* can be bought and eaten at any time of day but is very popular for breakfast or during the mid-morning, and is served with coffee.

CANTELO

This wedding bread is a traditional bread from the northern region of Portugal. The loaf is baked in a ring, and custom dictates that the bride and groom break the bread into pieces to give to their wedding guests with a glass of wine.

PAPO SECOS

These small white rolls are a popular breakfast bread all over Portugal. They have a soft white crumb and a delicious crust that is crisp without being hard. Like many breads from Portugal, they are baked with lots of steam which accounts for their good crust yet ensures that the crumb is light and airy.

RIGHT: Bolo do caco is a hearth bread like focaccia and fougasse.

ABOVE: If you live near a Portuguese baker, try caracas as an alternative to regular hamburger buns.

CARACAS

Caracas are similar in size and shape to *papo secos* but are more akin to an English or Scottish bap, batch-baked and cooked with less steam so they are softer and less crusty.

BOLO DO CACO

This flattish loaf is similar to the Spanish olive oil bread. It is another type of hearth bread, cooked on the sole of a very hot oven. It is best eaten very fresh with dressed salads or with other foods that have plenty of liquids that need mopping up.

MAIA BREAD

This is a long white loaf, normally made using a plain white dough. It is popular all over Portugal and is one of the better-known everyday breads, eaten with fish soups and salads, and Portuguese cheese.

BELOW: Maia bread is almost always a white loaf and has a good, slightly chewy crust.

GERMAN BREADS

There is an enormous range of German breads. Outside Germany – in Britain for instance – you could be forgiven for thinking that all German breads come in neat packages wrapped in cellophane. These are in fact the *kastenbrots* (box breads) and include the well-known pumpernickel. In Germany, however, and increasingly available throughout Europe and North America, there are also the German *krustenbrots* (crusty breads). These are the freshly baked breads, bought from a bakery or from the fresh bread counters at supermarkets, and they are as varied and delicious as the loaves to be found in the rest of continental Europe. The German word *brot* means either wheat or rye bread, with other breads named for the type of grain used in their making: oats, corn or barley.

KASTENBROTS

In the customary way that German words very often describe exactly what they mean, *kastenbrots* translates as "box bread". The bread is steam-baked for some 20 hours in an enclosed tin, which

BELOW: Pumpernickel is the best-known of the German kastenbrots.

results in a dense and heavy loaf which is both moist and crumbly with a chewy texture. It has a sour flavour but with a certain sweet, malty overtone and, unlike most breads, has a distinctive but not unpleasant after-taste. *Kastenbrots* are not breads to be eaten with wine, but are best enjoyed with a jug of cool German beer.

These breads almost invariably use rye flour (normally a wholemeal grain that can be coarsely or more finely ground according to the type of bread). The

dough uses a natural, sourdough leaven, which adds to the sour taste of the bread and complements the flavour of the rye, with its own earthy taste. The darkest *kastenbrots* contain only rye but wheat flour is added in varying proportions to give a loaf that is lighter in appearance, texture and flavour. Other grains, such as oats or barley, as well as sunflower and sesame seeds, are added to certain loaves, and there are therefore numerous variations on the basic theme. The bread always comes thinly sliced, wrapped in cellophane and clearly labelled. While moist in texture, the bread, with its sweet/sour yet dry flavour tastes best buttered or spread with a soft cheese. Savoury foods, such as smoked salmon, soused herring or German sausage, are most commonly served with the darker breads, but the lighter breads are excellent with marmalade or other sharply flavoured conserves.

PUMPERNICKEL

The best known of all the *kastenbrots*, pumpernickel is also the darkest of these breads. It is usually made with 100 per cent coarsely ground rye grain, and has an unmistakable sour, earthy flavour, but

LEFT: Vollkornbrot (left) is a 100 per cent rye bread, while roggenbrot (back) is slightly lighter, containing some wheat flour. Sonnenblumenbrot (right) is made with sunflower seeds, which give a lighter flavour and a good texture.

some are made with slightly less rye flour and a small amount of wheat flour. Like many German breads, pumpernickel is sometimes flavoured with caraway seeds.

VOLLKORNBROT OR SCHWARZBROT

This is another strongly flavoured bread, the names of which translate as "whole corn" or "black" bread. The whole "corn" in this instance is rye, which again is coarsely ground. The bread also contains molasses, adding to the dark colour and the malty flavour of the bread – which is probably one for devotees only.

ROGGENBROT

Roggen is German for rye, but this bread in fact often contains a small proportion of wheat flour, too. *Roggenbrot* is a dark oblong tin loaf with a hard crust that is sometimes encrusted with whole grains. In spite of the added wheat flour, this is still an intensely flavoured bread, best eaten with strong-tasting foods.

SONNENBLUMENBROT

Sunflower seeds give this bread a pleasant crunchy texture. *Sonnenblumenbrut* is made mainly using rye flour, but a small proportion of wheat flour together with the sunflower seeds makes this a more palatable loaf for those sampling *kastenbrot* for the first time.

WEISENKEIMBROT

This means "wheat germ bread" and it is made using the wheat germ, along with rye grain

ABOVE: Three krustenbrots: Black Forest (left), Bavarian rye (right) and roggenbrot.

and flour. *Grahamsbrot* uses a higher proportion of wholemeal flour, specifically the American-style Graham wholewheat flour.

MUESLIBROT

This is a multigrain *kastenbrot,* made using a muesli-style mix of cereals, chopped nuts and whole grains. It is a popular choice in Germany for those who want a healthy teabread that has plenty of texture and is not overly sweet.

KRUSTENBROTS

These crusty breads are the day-to-day breads of Germany, and are also popular in parts of Canada and in the American states around the Great Lakes, where German emigrés settled in the 1840s. In other European countries, German-style bakers import the flours from Germany or bake them using locally bought flours and meals, but sometimes import the sourdough culture from their native home. Many, although not all, German breads contain rye flour.

LEFT: Weisenkeimbrot (back) is made with both rye and wheat flours, while mueslibrot contains a mixture of cereals, nuts and whole grains.

ABOVE: Landbrot

BELOW: German square rye

and also partly to the long fermentation process. Like most German ryes, it too uses the sourdough principle and consequently has a noticeable yet mild, sour flavour. It is good with German meats and sausages or with creamy cheeses.

LANDBROT

This is a traditional country bread, made using a large proportion of wheat flour but with enough rye to give a pale, beige-coloured crumb. It has an excellent sweet/sour flavour, partly from the rye and partly from the buttermilk, which is used instead of milk or water. It comes in all sorts of shapes and sizes, sometimes with a floury crust and sometimes without. Inside, the bread is always open-textured and slightly chewy, and is good with soups and stews.

ROGGENBROT

Unlike the *kastenbrot* of the same name, this crusty bread contains only rye grain and rye flour. It is a robust, sourdough loaf with a thick, chewy crust.

GERMAN RYE BREAD

There are many varieties of this sturdy loaf, including the well-known Bavarian rye. Rye breads come in various shapes and sizes, but are most often tin or bloomer-shaped. The loaf typically has more rye than usual, but wheat flour is

Rye was once the main cereal in northern Europe. It tolerates the cooler dryer climatic conditions, and for centuries, while the more affluent enjoyed white bread made with imported wheat, the poor continued to eat bread made with the grain that was cheap and readily available. When wheat became relatively inexpensive in Germany white wheat flour was used by all but the very poorest, either by itself or with rye flour. There is consequently a great variety of German breads. Some are baked in tins, but the majority are baked on the floor of the oven and are evenly crusty.

RIGHT: German rye

GERMAN SQUARE RYE

This is an easily recognized bread: it is a large square loaf that is cross-hatched on top. It is often just known as German rye, but unlike other ryes of that name it has a pleasant, gentle flavour, due partly to the blend of rye and wheat flours, there too, for a lighter texture. Like many German breads, it is made by the sourdough method. The culture is made by mixing rye flour with water to produce just the right balance of acids to work the dough. Although these cultures can last for many years if fed and reinvigorated correctly, most bakers will start a new culture every week, mainly so that they – and you – know what you are getting.

A 100 per cent rye bread contains, as you might expect, only rye flour and is therefore suitable for anyone with an allergy to wheat. This, too, uses the sourdough method and has a dense texture and strong, sour flavour.

GEBILDBROTE (PICTURE BREAD)

Now something of a rarity, these breads can still be found in villages on festive occasions. The bread is moulded into complex shapes and patterns, normally with symbolic meanings. Loaves may be embossed with horses, deer, serpents, flowers and sheaves of wheat or they may be fashioned into shapes of men and women. The origin of this custom most likely dates from pagan times when bread would have been offered to appease the gods. Christianity also used breads in many rituals and many of the *gebildbrote* bear Christian symbols, such as crucifixes, loaves and fishes.

PRETZELS

Although extremely popular as snacks in America, and well known among the Jewish breads, pretzels are nevertheless German in origin. Like *gebildbrote*, pretzels have a symbolic meaning, which may have had its origins in pagan times. The distinctive knot shape is believed by some to have been a symbol for the solar cycle; others believe the crossed arms symbolize the Cross and that pretzels were originally made as a Lenten bread. Whatever the explanation, pretzels clearly have important significance in Germany and beyond – the same symbol of interlocking rings is the sign of a baker's shop throughout northern Europe.

Pretzels are almost always made using white flour and, according to a decree of 1256 in Landshut, it was a punishable

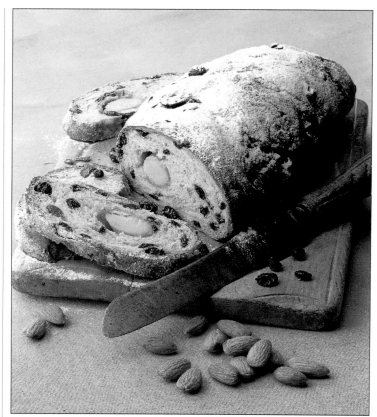

ABOVE: Stollen is a popular Christmas treat in many European countries. It is rich with fruit and often has a sweet marzipan centre.

offence for a baker to bake pretzels from anything but the finest white flour. Unlike the more familiar salted biscuits, German pretzels in many ways resemble a bagel. Along with the white flour, they contain yeast and milk and are poached, sprinkled liberally with sea salt and then baked until the crust is hard and golden. This salty, crunchy crust contrasts with the soft, sweet-flavoured crumb.

ROLLS

There is an enormous variety of German style rolls. Most are made from white flour and may be sprinkled with caraway or poppy seeds. *Semmel,* with their star-shaped design on top, and *Eiweckerl* are mainly served at breakfast.

STOLLEN

There are many German sweet breads but perhaps the best-known and -loved is stollen, sold almost everywhere as a treat around Christmas. It is an oval-shaped loaf, which tapers at each end. The shape is said to represent the infant Jesus wrapped in swaddling clothes. The bread is packed with sultanas, currants and mixed peel, and is usually spiced and enriched with eggs, butter and milk. Almonds may be finely chopped and added to the dough with the fruit, or they may be ground and made into a paste that is then rolled into the bread, giving it a sweet, moist centre. Stollen is unfailingly delicious, although it is predictably on the calorific side.

FOUR CEREAL BREAD

This dark, solid loaf is made using a blend of cereals but always including both rye and wheat.

BELOW: Four cereal bread.

GOLDGRAIN

Sometimes called a *multigrained* loaf, this baguette-shaped loaf is made using wheat, rye, barley, oats, soya, linseed, sunflower seeds, wheat bran, semolina and millet. For all this vast array of ingredients it is not unduly heavy and it has a texture not dissimilar to a Granary bread, with a wholesome, nutty flavour. Goldgrain sometimes is made with the addition of chopped walnuts. Both varieties are popular in health-conscious Germany and are becoming more easily available elsewhere. They are distributed by several producers.

BELOW: Mehrkorn is available as both a crusty bread and as a thinly sliced box bread.

GERMAN BREAD WITH CARAWAY SEEDS

Caraway is a favourite ingredient in German rye breads, adding its unmistakable aniseed flavour. Although often called "German rye with caraway" or "light rye with caraway", the bread does contain a large proportion of wheat flour, giving it a light texture and flavour.

KUGELHOPF

This bread belongs equally to the Alsace region of France and to Vienna in Austria. There are various ways of spelling *kugelhopf* and even more ways for making and baking it. In Alsace it is a savoury bread made with bacon, lard and/or fromage blanc and cream cheese. The German and Austrian *kugelhopf,* by contrast, is a yeasted brioche-style bread, made using sultanas and raisins and enriched with butter and eggs. A good *kugelhopf* has a delicious citrus flavour, provided by lemon rind and juice.

The *kugelhopf* is baked in a fluted mould with a central funnel, and the top billows out like a "kugel", or ball.

MEHRKORN

Mehrkorn means "more grain" and this bread is a multigrain loaf. The mixture of grains means that the bread is noticeably lighter than many of the principally rye breads.

AUSTRIAN BREADS

As you would expect, a large number of the most popular Austrian breads are similar, if not identical, to those of neighbouring Switzerland, Italy, and Germany. However, Austria may well have been responsible for many of the more elaborate continental breads. It was the Austrians who developed the *poolisch* or sponge method of leavening dough, also used in France. This was particularly popular for white breads or those using finer flours, and breads made by this method were noted for their excellent flavour. Not surprisingly, Vienna became the home of fine baking. Croissants are just one among many delicacies that may originally have come from the master bakers of Austria, although any French person will certainly disagree!

BAURNBROT

While Austria is paradise for all those who love rich breads and pastries, there are still country-style loaves to be found. Not least of these is *baurnbrot*, made using buckwheat and wheat flour and molasses, flavoured with caraway seeds and leavened using a rye sourdough starter. This makes for a robust and strongly flavoured loaf, which tastes best with simple foods, such as country cheeses, sausages and meats, or simply dunked in soup.

PRETZELS

Pretzels or brezeln, as they are known in Germany, are said to be derived from the Latin bracellae *or arms, referring to the crossed "arms" of dough inside the oval shape. This shape is also used for biscuits in Germany and Austria, and in Alsace the pretzel shape is part of the wrought iron emblem of quality that bakers display outside their shops.*

1 Lightly flour a baking sheet. Also grease 2 baking sheets. Cream the yeast for the yeast sponge with the water, then mix in the flour, cover with clear film and leave to stand at room temperature for 2 hours.

FOR THE YEAST SPONGE
7g/¼ oz fresh yeast
75ml/5 tbsp water
15ml/1 tbsp unbleached plain white flour
FOR THE DOUGH
7g/¼ oz fresh yeast
150ml/¼ pint/⅔ cup lukewarm water
75ml/5 tbsp lukewarm milk
400g/14oz/3½ cups unbleached white bread flour
7.5ml/1½ tsp salt
25g/1oz/2 tbsp butter, melted

FOR THE TOPPING
1 egg yolk
15ml/1 tbsp milk
sea salt or caraway seeds, for sprinkling

MAKES 12 PRETZELS

2 Mix the yeast for the dough with the water until dissolved, then stir in the milk. Sift 350g/12oz/3 cups of the flour and the salt into a large bowl. Add the yeast sponge mixture and the butter; mix for 3–4 minutes. Turn out on to a lightly floured surface and knead in the remaining flour to make a medium firm dough. Place in a lightly oiled bowl, cover with lightly oiled clear film and leave to rise, in a warm place, for 30 minutes, or until almost doubled in bulk

3 Turn out on to a lightly floured surface and knock back the dough. Knead into a ball, return to the bowl, re-cover and leave to rise for 30 minutes.

4 Turn out the dough on to a lightly floured surface. Divide the dough into 12 equal pieces and form into balls. Take one ball of dough and cover the remainder with a dish towel. Roll into a thin stick 46cm/18in long and about 1cm/½ in thick in the middle and thinner at the ends. Bend each end of the dough stick into a horseshoe. Cross over and place the ends on top of the thick part of the pretzel. Repeat with the remaining dough balls.

5 Place on the floured baking sheet to rest for 10 minutes. Meanwhile, preheat the oven to 190°C/375°F/Gas 5. Bring a large saucepan of water to the boil, then reduce to a simmer. Add the pretzels to the simmering water in batches, about 2–3 at a time and poach for about 1 minute. Drain the pretzels on a dish towel and place on the greased baking sheets, spaced well apart.

6 Mix the egg yolk and milk together and brush this glaze over the pretzels. Sprinkle with sea salt or caraway seeds and bake the pretzels for 25 minutes, or until they are deep golden. Transfer to a wire rack to cool.

PUMPERNICKEL

This famous German bread is extremely dense and dark, with an intense flavour. It is baked very slowly and although cooked in the oven, it is more like a steamed bread than a baked one.

450g/1lb/4 cups rye flour
225g/8oz/2 cups wholemeal flour
115g/4oz/⅔ cup bulgur wheat
10ml/2 tsp salt
30ml/2 tbsp molasses
850ml/1 pint 8fl oz/3½ cups warm water
15ml/1 tbsp vegetable oil

MAKES 2 LOAVES

COOK'S TIP
This bread improves on keeping. Keep for at least 24 hours double-wrapped inside a plastic bag or greaseproof paper and foil before slicing.

1 Lightly grease two 18 × 9cm/7 × 3½ in loaf tins. Mix the rye flour, wholemeal flour, bulgur wheat and salt together in a large bowl.

2 Mix the molasses with the warm water and add to the flours with the vegetable oil. Mix together to form a dense mass.

3 Place in the prepared tins, pressing well into the corners. Cover with lightly oiled clear film and leave in a warm place for 18–24 hours.

4 Preheat the oven to 110°C/225°F/ Gas ¼. Cover the tins tightly with foil. Fill a roasting tin with boiling water and place a rack on top.

5 Place the tins on top of the rack and transfer very carefully to the oven. Bake the loaves for 4 hours. Increase the oven temperature to 160°C/325°F/Gas 3. Top up the water in the roasting tin if necessary, uncover the loaves and bake for a further 30–45 minutes, or until the loaves feel firm and the tops are crusty.

6 Leave to cool in the tins for 5 minutes, then turn out on to a wire rack to cool completely. Serve cold, very thinly sliced, with cold meats.

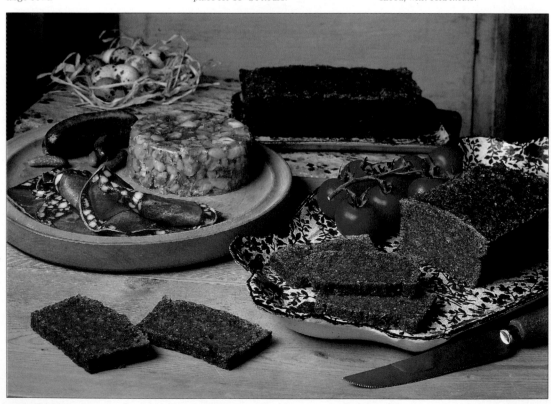

DUTCH BREADS

KORNKRACKER

Kornkracker can refer to either loaves or rolls. The bread is popular throughout Germany and Holland. The word means "cracked corn" and the bread is made with cracked whole grain wheat, together with malted wheat and seeds.

DUTCH FRUIT LOAF

This lightly malted Granary loaf rich with fruit and sprinkled with sugar is popular with coffee at any time of the day. It is also a favourite treat for children and is sometimes served with a mild cheese, such as Edam or Gouda.

RIGHT: Kornkracker

DUTCH CRISPBREADS

The Dutch enjoy crispbreads almost as much as the Scandinavians. They are usually served at breakfast, eaten with cheese or smoked hams, or spread with jam or marmalade. The round breads that are commonly available outside The Netherlands are baked until completely crisp. They have a unique, vaguely sweet flavour, which is surprisingly good with savoury foods. Dutch crispbreads come in cylindrical packets and are generally available everywhere.

FRISIAN SUGAR LOAF

This unusual sweet bread is made using whole sugar lumps that melt as the bread is baked to give delicious pockets of sweetness, which contrast with the cinnamon in the soft white crumb.

DUTCH ROGGEBROOD

Holland also has its own varieties of *kastenbrots* and *krustenbrots*. This box-style bread is similar to the German *roggenbrot,* made with rye flour and leavened using the sourdough method. It often contains molasses and is consequently very dark with a strong malty taste.

Holland even has its own pumpernickel which, like the German variety, contains 100 per cent rye flour. The Dutch pumpernickel is a little sweeter than the German version, but with the same strong flavour. It is not for the faint-hearted!

ABOVE: Dutch fruit bread

RIGHT: Dutch crispbreads – popular everywhere.

SWISS BREADS

One of the least accessible and smallest countries of Western Europe, Switzerland has an extraordinary wealth of unusual and tasty breads. There are probably two explanations for this. First, the mountains that cover 70 per cent of Switzerland mean that, until quite recently, villages have existed in relative isolation, and rural traditions, such as baking and bread making, have endured, undiluted by commercialization and mass markets. The other significant factor is that four of Switzerland's five neighbours (the fifth is tiny Liechtenstein) – France, Germany, Italy and Austria – are home to most of the best breads in the world.

As well as producing many loaves that will be familiar to its neighbours, Switzerland has borrowed some of the best breads to develop its own specialities. These, too, reflect the influence of near neighbours and, in common with the pattern elsewhere, rye breads are baked in the north; soft white loaves in the south and east.

BELOW: Crusty bauerruch

APFELNUSSBROT

The name denotes the Germanic origins of this unusual bread, but it seems to be a distillation of a variety of traditions from France as well as Germany. The round, crusty loaf is made from a blend of grains including wheat, rye, barley and spelt, which points to a German influence, yet the apples and walnuts seem typically French and the bread is not unlike the *pain aux pommes* from France. The best loaves are said to be found in Valais, in the south of the country.

BANGELI

This crusty loaf is a cross between the French baguette and the long white loaves of Germany. It comes from Basel, a Swiss town on the border of France and Germany, which perhaps explains its hybrid appearance. It is a long loaf that looks rather rustic, with seven or eight horizontal slashes and a thick, floury crust. The bread is often cut into chunks to serve with fondue.

BAUERRUCH

Swiss bakers take an enormous pride in their work and some of the Swiss breads are beautifully crafted, for example the *bauerruch*, which is a rounded crusty loaf shaped in a swirl like a turban or a seashell. It is a fairly dense white or brown bread with a thick, golden crust.

PANIS LUNATIS

This means moon bread. In Switzerland, some believe it was the precursor to the croissant. Indeed moon bread was baked as long ago as the 8th century. Today Swiss bakers sell croissants only, but they always claim to have invented them.

SAKO

Although some wheat is grown in Switzerland, neither the soil nor the climate favour agriculture and the little wheat that was coaxed from the land was frequently blended with other grains to make tasty and healthy loaves. The *sako* is a round multigrain loaf made with eight different cereals. It is usually risen in a floured basket, then turned out for baking. *Sako* is often slashed off-centre across the top and is generally sprinkled with cracked wheat or rolled oats. It is a somewhat dense loaf, excellent for mopping up soups.

SWISS PEASANT LOAF

There are many variations on the theme of a Swiss rustic loaf, but most are round, free-form loaves, made with a blend of wheat and rye flours but with cracked rye and chopped walnuts giving the loaves a pleasant texture.

VOGEL LOAF

This is a proprietary Swiss loaf that is renowned for its healthy properties. It was developed over 30 years ago by a Swiss nutritionist, Dr Alfred Vogel. A multi-grain bread, it contains kibbled wheat, rye grain and bran, giving it a high-fibre

ABOVE: The attractive and simple Swiss peasant loaf.

RIGHT: Healthy Vogel loaf

RIGHT: Zupfe is also known as Swiss braid.

tradition of plaiting bread came is not known, only that it is extremely old. It may have symbolized the braid of hair offered by the wife or widow of a warrior to ensure his safe return from battle. Shaped into a round, it could have represented the course of the sun, while the crescent may have signified the moon. The Swiss plaited breads are almost always yeast-leavened, made using white wheat flour, and may be plaited with three or more strands of dough. There is really no limit to the baker's art and the Swiss have a reputation for their skill with shaping bread.

GIPFELTEIG

These are essentially tiny croissants and are quite the best thing to eat for breakfast if you are visiting Switzerland. They are so small – three or four will fit comfortably in your hand – and so delicious, that it is easy to consume far too many before you decide you have probably had enough! They resemble, and may be identical to, the tiny croissants you will be served in the Alsace area and other parts of western France and, like them, the bakers use lard as well as butter in the dough to give a texture that is very soft. *Gipfelteig* are best eaten fresh and warm as they are, or spread with a little apricot jam or some tangy orange marmalade.

WEGGLITAG

These little rolls are often served for breakfast along with *gipfelteig*. The small, oval white rolls are always glazed with beaten egg and notched across the top with scissors to give a crenellated effect and a crunchy crust.

content, which is one of its main selling points. The whole and cracked grain gives the loaf plenty of texture, yet the flavour is not too strong, making it a popular choice for those who like their fibre to be subtle rather than overpowering.

ZUPFE (ZOPF)

Known variously as *zupfe*, *zopf* or Swiss braid, this is a plaited loaf made from a rich dough, which typically contains soured cream or milk, egg and butter. It has a glossy crust and beautifully light crumb. Like its neighbours, Austria and Germany, Switzerland has a great affection for these rich doughs, which are shaped, plaited or twisted into spectacular loaves. This is where the tradition of the Jewish *challah* – another plaited loaf – is believed to have evolved. Exactly from where the

ABOVE AND BELOW: Wegglitag and gipfelteig are a great way to start the day.

NORDIC BREADS

Rye, oats and barley were once the only crops that would grow in the cooler climate and acidic soils of northern Europe. While wheat was imported for the prosperous, for the majority of people bread was inevitably made using one type or a blend of these cereals. Rye, which contains gluten, was favoured for leavened bread since it would rise and produce a lighter loaf. In Norway, however, where there was a fondness for unleavened bread, oats and barley and sometimes pea-flour were for many centuries the favoured ingredients for making their popular *flatbrød*.

Nowadays, wheat can be grown in the more temperate parts of Denmark and Sweden, and of course, being widely imported, white breads are commonly available. Traditionally, the festive breads have always been made from the finest white flours. Scandinavians set great store by their festivals and each year buy or make their Christmas and Easter breads, along with a host of other breads made for celebrations in between.

White breads are particularly popular in the cities, but the Scandinavians continue to love their dark rye breads and visitors will find that there is a wide choice of breads – from the weird and wonderful breads of Lapland to the *flatbrøds* of Norway, and the rich pumpernickel breads baked in Denmark.

RIGHT: Danish rye bread is lighter in texture and colour than German ryes.

DANISH BREADS

RYE BREAD

There are numerous types of Danish rye breads and you will need to sample a few to discover the ones you like best. Danish ryes tend to be lighter and sweeter than most German ryes. Molasses and malt extract are popular ingredients, adding to the dark colour, but this is tempered by the greater proportion of white wheat flour. Danish ryes also tend to contain a proportion of fat, either buttermilk or butter or both. This helps to

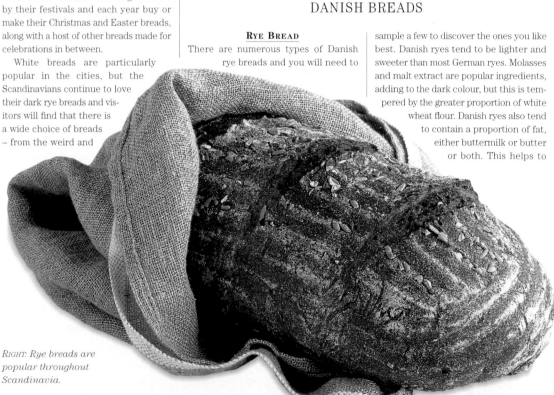

RIGHT: Rye breads are popular throughout Scandinavia.

RIGHT: The plaited tresse

preserve the loaf and gives a richer and more open-textured bread. Danish ryes are the popular breads for *smørrebrød* (the equivalent to the Swedish *smörgåsbord*), the buffet-style open sandwiches topped with meats and cheese.

KERNEBROD

A seeded loaf, normally made with a Granary meal, sprinkled liberally with sunflower seeds and linseeds.

TRESSE

This is a plaited white loaf, enriched with milk, eggs and butter. It may be scattered freely with poppy or sesame seeds and is popular throughout the year, although at one time this loaf was probably made for special occasions.

DANISH FESTIVE FRUIT LOAF (JULEKAGE)

This is one of the most famous of all the Danish Christmas loaves. Christmas is a hugely important festival in all parts of Scandinavia, not only for its Christian significance, but also because it heralds the halfway point of the long Nordic winter. Similar breads, filled with fruit, nuts and spices, and enriched with butter and eggs, are made all over Scandinavia. *Julekage* is traditionally spiced with vanilla and cardamom. Crushed sugar is then sprinkled over the top before baking and, finally, icing sugar is drizzled over the bread when it is cooked.

CARNIVAL BUNS (FASTERLAVNSBOILLER)

Any Dane will be able to tell you about these treats, which they will remember from their childhood and probably now make for their own children. They are traditionally made on the Monday before Shrove Tuesday, which is celebrated not only with breads and cakes but also with some games, including "beating a cat off the barrel", which involves children chasing each other and which thankfully has nothing to do with cats, in spite of its name. The little square or round buns are something like a cross between a bread and an English Yorkshire pudding, made with white flour and yeast and enriched with egg, butter and milk. Carnival buns are flavoured with cardamom and filled with almond paste and sometimes with chopped peel, and are normally liberally dusted with icing sugar.

SMØRREBRØD

The word simply means "buttered bread" but the famous Danish open sandwiches are so much more than that. Delicious toppings – their ingredients limited only by the imagination of the cook – are laid on thin slices of bread. The aim of the exercise is to produce a snack that is as appealing to the eye as it is to the stomach, and the results are as colourful as they are good to eat. Danish sour rye bread is the preferred base, although for some more delicate toppings, such as smoked salmon, baby shrimps, prawns or lobster, a crusty white bread is sometimes used. Fish and shellfish are favourite toppings, one of the most popular choices being pickled herring with marinated onion rings. Liver paste, salami, cheeses (including the famous blue cheese of Denmark), roast pork, hard-boiled eggs – the list of potential toppings is apparently limitless, as is the Danes' capacity for enjoying their favourite lunchtime snack.

NORWEGIAN AND SWEDISH BREADS

NORWEGIAN FLAT BREAD

Flatbrød is the oldest of all the Norwegian breads and was, until fairly recently, the bread most commonly eaten by the people of Norway. A long time ago these wafer-thin crispbreads would have been made with any cereal that was to hand – mostly oats, rye, barley or pea-flour, or a mixture of all these. The unleavened dough would have been rolled into very thin, large circles and baked on a griddle or on a stone over an open fire. The breads were known to last for months, even up to a year, and would be stored on the beams over the kitchen. These days the breads are factory-baked and sold ready-cut into convenient rectangles. Some bakers, however, continue to make their own, and in parts of Norway the large breads are served at harvest meals, dampened with a little water so they become pliable and can be wrapped around Norwegian sweet cheese or other suitable pieces of food.

NORWEGIAN WHOLEMEAL BREAD

This fine bread is made with whole wheat kernels, skimmed milk, yeast, cottage cheese and wholemeal flour, and is topped with crushed wheat.

RIGHT: Lomper is a soft flat bread cooked on a griddle.

LEFT: Flatbrød

LIMPA

Limpa is a Swedish favourite – a leavened rye loaf, sweetened with molasses or honey, flavoured with orange and lightly spiced with cardamom, cumin, fennel and anise. Since wheat flour makes up the greater proportion of flour, the loaf is not as heavy as some rye loaves, although it has the typical dense yet crumbly texture of rye breads. *Vortlimpa* is a far darker loaf than *limpa,* containing a greater proportion of rye flour together with the dark molasses. It, too, contains orange rind, either grated or finely chopped, and can also be made with ground or whole fennel seeds. In spite of the sweet molasses, this dark, savoury loaf is intended to be eaten with soft cheese or salted herring.

ROGBROD

Røgbrød is the traditional rye bread of Sweden, made in large flat loaves and often containing molasses, which has been valued by Sweden and the other Baltic states since it was first imported. Unlike the flat Norwegian ryes, *røgbröd* is a leavened bread, traditionally made using a sourdough method, but also using normal yeast. Buttermilk is often used instead of ordinary milk, adding to the acidic flavour of the bread, which is also flavoured with fennel or caraway seeds.

Ragbröd is much the same as *røgbröd* – made of rye and often containing molasses – but is shaped into a ring by being rolled out into a flat round and then having a hole cut in the middle. Traditionally, *ragbröd* would have been looped across the kitchen with string, and even today you may see them displayed in such a way in some bakeries.

LEFT: Swedish krisprolls

SWEDISH CARDAMOM BRAID
This is a delicious sweet fruit bread, made with white flour, enriched with milk, eggs and butter and spiced with the distinctive flavour of cardamom.

SWEDISH CARAWAY BREAD
This is a half-sweet, half-savoury white bread, made with a little sugar and butter, yet given a subtle savoury flavour by the caraway seeds.

ST LUCIA ROLLS
Throughout Scandinavia, the days leading up to Christmas are as much a time of festivity as Christmas Day itself. St Lucia Day (13 December) is celebrated widely in Sweden. Children dress up in white and visit each other's homes. They wear crowns of glowing candles, symbolizing the light that will come once winter is over. The favourite food for the children are the little St Lucia rolls, traditionally made with saffron and enriched with eggs, butter and milk. Each bread is shaped in the letter "S" and topped with a raisin.

KNACKERBROD
Sweeter than the Finnish *knackebrod*, these Swedish flat breads are made with rolled oats and taste a little like sweet Scottish oatcakes. Unlike Scottish oatcakes, however, they are leavened using bicarbonate of soda and buttermilk, and are baked in the oven.

SCANDINAVIAN STAR
This unusual and pretty bread is a modern adaptation of some of the best Scandinavian baking traditions. It is made using a blend of white and Granary flours but its fine flavour is due mainly to the sponge method of making the dough, which allows the flavours to develop, and the longer-than-usual rising. Sunflower seeds and linseeds are added for flavour and the bread is liberally sprinkled with sesame seeds before being stamped into its distinctive star shape. The bread has a good crisp crust, while the crumb is soft with a rich nutty flavour. It makes an excellent breaking bread, which is appropriate since pulling off pieces of bread is preferred in Scandinavia to slicing bread conventionally.

SCANDINAVIAN CRISPBREADS
There are many Scandinavian crispbreads, ranging from crisp rusks to wafer-thin biscuits. Norwegian crispbreads are made mainly with whole rye, although there are also many made with a blend of wheat flours. *Krisprolls* are popular in Sweden, eaten at almost any time of the day, but particularly at breakfast. They are baked until entirely crisp and have a noticeably sweet flavour.

LEFT: The Scandinavian star bread, with its liberal sprinkling of sesame seeds, looks attractive and has an excellent flavour.

FINNISH AND ARCTIC BREADS

FINNISH KNACKEBROD

This thin, biscuit-like bread with its characteristic central hole is made using a blend of rye and corn. Freshly made *knackebrod* are crisp and are delicious with a fresh goat's cheese or smoked salmon. *Wiborgs kringla* are also from Finland and are similar in many ways to Germany's pretzels: the entwined strands, like a lover's knot, appear in bakers' shop signs in Finland. The enriched yeast bread was traditionally baked on straw, and even today the bread is cooked in a similar way, and it is a feature of the bread that bits of straw need to be pulled off the bottom before it is eaten.

FINNISH EASTER BREAD

For most of Scandinavia, and certainly for those who were better off, most of the original festive breads were made from what was considered the best flour, namely white wheat flour. In the poorer villages and towns, however, most people had to make do with what they could find – usually rye, barley and oatmeal. For festivals special

LEFT: Icelandic bread

breads were made to celebrate using only these three cereals. Easter bread was a particular favourite, moulded in a traditional round, and made with yogurt and honey or molasses and packed with raisins, sultanas and nuts. Easter bread is unlikely to be widely available in the cities, but should you travel through villages at the right time of year, you may find these dark specialities with their shiny tops.

HALKAKA

This heavy black rye bread was once the only food for a number of Finnish peasants during the winter. Extremely large loaves were baked and then gradually eaten over the next few months until the bread was finished and it was time to bake once more.

RIESKA

Further north in Finland, the leavened breads give way to hard flat loaves. *Rieska* is a Finnish word and comes from Lapland, a region that extends across the northern parts of Norway, Sweden and Finland, and most of which is within the Arctic Circle. *Rieska* are round breads, mostly fairly small and rather flattish. They are normally made with oats or barley, but can also be made with potatoes or any starchy food. Although there is no wheat or rye to raise the dough, they do use a little yeast or baking powder, which makes them slightly less dense.

ICELANDIC BREAD

Most Icelandic breads are based on rye. Various loaves are made, from the crusty loaf with open crumb pictured above to the pancake-like *flatbrauð*, which are enjoyed with *skyr*, a fresh curd cheese that resembles yogurt.

POLAR FLAT BREAD

Called "polar rounds" or "polar thins", these small breads are easily available, sold in many large supermarkets or in delicatessens as a style of crispbread. They contain a mixture of rye and wheat flours and have a pleasant, slightly nutty flavour. They go well with strong-flavoured cheese, such as goat's cheese.

ABOVE: Polar flat breads are now made commercially.

FOR THE STARTER
60ml/4 tbsp lukewarm milk
60ml/4 tbsp lukewarm water
7g/¹/₄ oz fresh yeast
100g/3³/₄oz/scant 1 cup unbleached
white bread flour

FOR THE DOUGH
15g/¹/₂ oz fresh yeast
500ml/17fl oz/generous 2 cups
lukewarm water
450g/1lb/4 cups rye flour
225g/8oz/2 cups unbleached white
bread flour
15ml/1 tbsp salt
milk, for glazing
caraway seeds, for sprinkling

MAKES 1 LARGE LOAF

VARIATION
This bread can be shaped into one
large round or oval loaf, if preferred.

SUNSHINE LOAF

Scandinavia, Land of the Midnight Sun, has numerous breads based on rye.
This splendid table centrepiece is made with a blend of rye and white flours,
the latter helping to lighten the bread.

1 Combine the milk and water for the
starter in a large bowl. Mix in the yeast
until dissolved. Gradually add the bread
flour, stirring it with a metal spoon.

2 Cover the bowl with clear film and
leave the mixture in a warm place for
3–4 hours, or until well risen, bubbly
and starting to collapse.

3 Mix the yeast for the dough with
60ml/4 tbsp of the water until creamy,
then stir in the remaining water.
Gradually mix into the starter to dilute
it. Gradually mix in the rye flour to form
a smooth batter. Cover with lightly oiled
clear film and leave in a warm place, for
3–4 hours, or until well risen.

4 Stir the bread flour and salt into the
batter to form a dough. Turn on to a
lightly floured surface and knead for
5 minutes until smooth and elastic.
Place in a lightly oiled bowl, cover with
lightly oiled clear film and leave to rise,
in a warm place, for about 1 hour, or
until doubled in bulk.

5 Knock back on a lightly floured
surface. Cut the dough into 5 equal
pieces. Roll one piece into a 50cm/20in
"sausage" and roll up into a spiral shape.

6 Cut the remaining pieces of dough in
half and shape each one into a 20cm/8in
rope. Place in a circle on a large baking
sheet, spaced equally apart, like rays of
the sun, and curl the ends round,
leaving a small gap in the centre. Place
the spiral shape on top. Cover with
lightly oiled clear film and leave to rise,
in a warm place, for 30 minutes.

7 Meanwhile, preheat the oven to 230°C/
450°F/Gas 8. Brush the bread with milk,
sprinkle with caraway seeds and bake
for 30 minutes, or until lightly browned.
Transfer to a wire rack to cool.

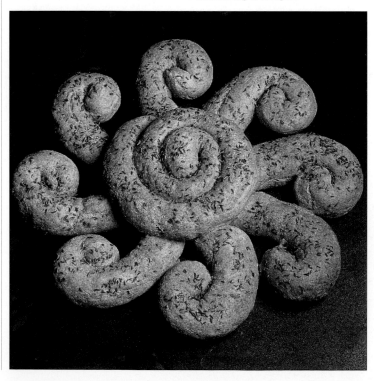

SAVOURY DANISH CROWN

Filled with golden onions and cheese, this butter-rich bread ring is quite irresistible and needs no accompaniment.

1 Lightly grease a baking sheet. Sift the flour and salt together into a large bowl. Rub in 40g/1½ oz/3 tbsp of the butter. Mix the yeast with the milk and water. Add to the flour with the egg and mix to a soft dough.

2 Turn out on to a lightly floured surface and knead for 10 minutes until smooth and elastic. Place in a lightly oiled bowl, cover with lightly oiled clear film or slide into an oiled polythene bag and leave to rise, in a warm place, for about 1 hour, or until doubled in bulk.

3 Knock back and turn out on to a lightly floured surface. Roll out into an oblong about 1cm/½ in thick.

4 Dot half the remaining butter over the top two-thirds of the dough. Fold the bottom third up and the top third down and seal the edges. Turn by 90 degrees and repeat with the remaining butter. Fold and seal as before. Cover the dough with lightly oiled clear film and leave to rest for about 15 minutes.

5 Turn by a further 90 degrees. Roll and fold again without any butter. Repeat once more. Wrap in lightly oiled clear film and leave to rest in the fridge for 30 minutes.

6 Meanwhile, heat the oil for the filling. Add the onions and cook for 10 minutes until soft and golden. Remove from the heat and stir in the breadcrumbs, almonds, Parmesan and seasoning.

7 Add half the beaten egg to the breadcrumb mixture and bind together.

8 Roll out the dough on a lightly floured surface into a rectangle measuring 56 × 23cm/22 × 9in. Spread with the filling to within 2cm/¾ in of the edges, then roll up like a Swiss roll from one long side. Using a very sharp knife, cut in half lengthways. Plait together with the cut sides up and shape into a ring. Place on the prepared baking sheet, cover with lightly oiled clear film and leave to rise, in a warm place, for 30 minutes.

9 Meanwhile, preheat the oven to 200°C/400°F/Gas 6. Brush the remaining beaten egg over the dough. Sprinkle with sesame seeds and Parmesan cheese and bake for 40–50 minutes, or until golden. Transfer to a wire rack to cool slightly if serving warm, or cool completely to serve cold, cut into slices.

350g/12oz/3 cups unbleached white bread flour
5ml/1 tsp salt
185g/6½ oz/generous ¾ cup butter, softened
20g/¾ oz fresh yeast
200ml/7fl oz/scant 1 cup mixed lukewarm milk and water
1 egg, lightly beaten

FOR THE FILLING
30ml/2 tbsp sunflower oil
2 onions, finely chopped
40g/1½ oz/¾ cup fresh breadcrumbs
25g/1oz/¼ cup ground almonds
50g/2oz/½ cup freshly grated Parmesan cheese
1 egg, lightly beaten
salt and freshly ground black pepper

FOR THE TOPPING
15ml/1 tbsp sesame seeds
15ml/1 tbsp freshly grated Parmesan cheese

MAKES 1 LARGE LOAF

EASTERN EUROPEAN AND RUSSIAN BREADS

In the cool latitudes of northern Europe, rye, buckwheat and barley were the principal cereals for centuries. Large dark breads made from these flours were not only the staple food, but during severe famine were often the only food for all but the most wealthy. "If we have bread and *kvas* (beer) what more do we need?" goes a Russian saying. Links with southern Europe meant that wheat flour gradually became popular, at first only among the aristocracy but later filtering through to the general population, where the flour was especially used for festive bread and cakes. Today, thanks to genetic manipulation, wheat is widely grown in Russia, Poland and other parts of eastern Europe, but the fondness for breads made from rye and buckwheat continues to this day and these traditional breads are still the mainstay for rural communities.

BLINIS

Although not strictly breads, these little buckwheat pancakes were the equivalent of festive sweet breads in a country where buckwheat rather than wheat was the principal crop. Buckwheat was widely cultivated in Russia in the past. At *Maslenitsa*, the week before

RIGHT: Polish rye bread

LEFT: Polish wholemeal rye uses wholemeal flour with a proportion of rye.

Lent, large numbers of blinis were consumed. They are just as popular now, eaten at any time of the year, most famously with *smetana* (a soured cream) and caviare, although also delicious with crème fraîche and smoked salmon. Blinis resemble in shape and size a Scotch pancake, but are normally far darker in colour with a savoury, slightly bitter flavour from the buckwheat flour. The most authentic blinis are made entirely of buckwheat but many are now a compromise with a blend of buckwheat and plain flour. The best blinis are yeast-risen, made using buttermilk or yogurt. Shop-bought blinis may have used baking powder instead and some contain so little buckwheat flour that they hardly merit the name "blini".

Pre-wrapped bought pancakes are best heated slightly in the microwave or wrapped in a cloth in the oven, so that they warm up without drying out.

BARLEY BREAD

Barley bread has long been baked in regions stretching from Finland to the shores of the Black Sea in the Ukraine. Barley made a change from the dark rye breads although, since it contains no gluten, loaves were consequently dense and heavy. Even today, many of the barley breads from the countries around the Baltic Sea are sturdy loaves, made with a blend of barley and wholemeal flour. The bread is generally moist and chewy. Cabbage leaves are sometimes used to line the baking tins, a time-honoured trick which keeps the crust moist.

POLISH RYE

As the name implies, this is made from rye, although some wheat flour is generally added. This bread, however, is made from refined rye meal, unlike Polish black rye which uses a coarser rye and wheat meal. Although they might sound not particularly appetizing, both breads are pleasantly flavoured.

ABOVE: Once the basic loaf for all poor families, Polish sourdough is now baked by craft bakers and is enjoyed by all bread enthusiasts.

RIGHT: Caraway seeds give Polish caraway a noticeable aniseed flavour.

POLISH BLACK BREAD

This is a large flattish and round bread, eaten in Poland, Lithuania and Latvia. Wheat flour is added to give some volume to the loaf, but it is principally made with buckwheat and has a distinctive, rather bitter flavour.

POLISH SOURDOUGH

This is a classic northern peasant-style rye bread. Originally, oats and barley may well have been added to the rye to make a loaf that would feed the family for as long as possible. Each household would take its grain to be milled and the bread would then be set to rise in proving troughs. The blend of grain plus the use of troughs gave a noticeably different flavour and texture to each loaf, from family to family and even from loaf to loaf.

POLISH CARAWAY BREAD

A traditional Polish medium rye bread, this is made with rye and wheat flour flavoured with caraway seeds.

ESTONIAN RYE

This is a sourdough bread made entirely with rye. It is a tin-shaped bread with a distinctive flavour arising from both the rye and the natural leaven.

SWEET PUMPERNICKEL

There are many styles of pumpernickel breads, all made entirely or principally from rye.

RUSSIAN BRAIDED BREAD

Braided yeasted loaves made using white flour are among the most familiar breads of eastern Europe. They are similar, and sometimes identical, to the Jewish *challah* since this part of Europe was home to many Jewish people. Many of these spectacular breads are enriched with milk, eggs and butter and are made as festive breads for special occasions. Others are plainer, sometimes using milk to obtain a softer crust, and are frequently sprinkled with poppy seeds.

RUSSIAN BLACK BREAD

Bread was by far the most important food in Russia until this century. In the 19th century, the Russian peasant ate on average 1.5kg/3–3½ lb of bread a day and even more at harvest time. White breads are now popular in Moscow and other large cities but it is the ryes that are the best-known and -loved of Russian breads. There are numerous types of black breads, varying in colour, density and sour/sweet flavour. Molasses, favoured throughout the Baltic States, is frequently added and originally the breads would have been made on the sourdough principle, although some today are yeast-leavened. Many are similar to German rye breads, since techniques and styles cross borders as easily as weather. A classic Russian black bread, however, is usually made with an equal blend of rye and wheat flour, using a sourdough starter. It

ABOVE: Estonian rye is one of the few tin breads baked in this region.

RIGHT: Russian black bread owes its dark colour to molasses and rye.

is spiced and oven bottom-baked. A round loaf, it has an attractive, coarse top. It is normally roughly broken rather than cut and is often eaten with soups and stews. In the Ukraine a version of a black rye bread is known as *chenyi khilb,* which is another large round loaf.

ROSSISKY

This is among the better-known Russian rye breads and is now made and sold outside Russia in some supermarkets, delicatessens and healthfood shops. It is 100 per cent rye bread, made using a sourdough starter, and has a distinctive yet pleasant flavour.

BORODINSKY

This small but compact loaf, traditionally flavoured with crushed coriander seeds, is becoming increasingly available outside Russia. Consequently, it represents, for many, the essence of Russian bread.

The story goes that the wife of a Russian general, Marshal Mikhail Kutuzov, made this sweet, aromatic bread for the army, which was defending Borodino, outside Moscow, from the onslaught of Napoleon's army. Although Napoleon then entered Moscow, the French were shortly forced to withdraw, which led to Napoleon's downfall. The Battle of Borodino thus became enshrined in Russian history and the bread was named

to remember both the eventual victory and the 42,000 men who lost their lives.

The Borodinsky loaf is baked, like the German box breads, in a sealed container; but unlike them it is cooked for only some 2½ hours, and uncovered for the final 15–30 minutes so that the bread is slightly risen with a firm crust. It is made either entirely with dark rye or with a blend of rye and wheatmeal. Barleymeal is also often used, giving an earthy flavour, while buttermilk or yogurt is also occasionally added and enhances the natural sour-dough flavour. Molasses, however, is traditionally used and malt is frequently added so that the bread acquires a sweet flavour, albeit with distinct sour/savoury overtones. Borodinsky is the most expensive and most popular of the Russian rye breads, and is served thinly sliced with strongly flavoured fish, such as pickled herring or smoked salmon.

RUSSIAN POTATO BREAD WITH CARAWAY SEEDS

Potatoes were another mainstay for the Russian peasant; breads were often made by using a mixture of a grain and potatoes that had been cooked and mashed. If the mixture included wheat, a flattish but loaf-shaped bread could be made. Caraway seeds were a popular flavouring.

HUNGARIAN CHRISTMAS BREAD

Called *makos es dios kalacs* in Hungarian, this is a popular festive enriched white bread, with the dough rolled around poppy seeds and raisins.

BALABUSKY

These little rolls speckled with caraway seeds are a speciality of the Ukraine, a region known for the variety of its breads. The rolls combine rye and wheat flours in varying proportions, but are made with soured cream, which gives a pleasant acidic flavour. Soured cream and curd cheese are an inheritance from the Tartars who invaded Russia and the Ukraine from Asia in the 13th century. The liking for soured cream, used in bread making and served with bread, is a feature of much eastern European cooking.

KOLACH (KALACH)

Kolach (kalach) is a sweet yeasted white bread, popular at Christmas in Bulgaria and Russia and especially in St Petersburg where it was said it should only be made from the water transported to the city from the Moskva river. It is normally plaited, although in the Ukraine and Moldova it is often formed into a round, like the sun – a reminder of warmer days to come.

KULICH

Kulich is the traditional Russian Easter cake. Apparently, in Tsarist Russia

RIGHT: Rossisky (back) and Borodinsky (front) are the cream of Russian breads.

labourers were not permitted to walk through the kitchen in case their heavy steps caused the dough to fall or the bread to collapse in the oven. The bread is similar to a brioche, made with white flour, eggs, butter and milk and rich with raisins, candied peel, angelica and chopped almonds. The tall, round bread is either glazed or iced and then decorated with glacé cherries, angelica or crystallized fruit. It is served, unusually, by slicing off the top and then slicing horizontally again for eating. The top is then replaced to keep the cake fresh for as long as possible.

The cake was also baked for Remembrance Monday, which is the Russian equivalent to All Souls' Day (2 November), when traditionally it would have been taken to the church in order to be blessed by the priest.

KRENDEL

Krendel or *kolindet* is a popular Russian sweet bread. With its intertwining loops, its shape is reminiscent of a pretzel and, similarly, has a significance that has been lost over the years. These breads were popular for birthdays and to celebrate name-days. They were also given to children on Christmas Eve so they may have been connected with the winter solstice. They are yeast-

RIGHT: Ukrainian rye is hugely popular wherever these Slav people have settled.

leavened, made with white flour and enriched with eggs, butter and cream. The breads have a deliciously soft, cake-like consistency and are sometimes served for tea in restaurants or at a *chaikhana* (tea house).

CZECHOSLOVAKIAN HOSKA

Another festive bread, this braided loaf is often decorated with whole almonds and then glazed with egg before and during cooking, so that it bakes to a beautiful golden hue. The bread is quite spectacular and no mean feat for the baker. The three tiers of braids are made successively smaller so that the braids balance on top of each other.

UKRAINIAN RYE

The Ukraine is renowned for its huge variety of breads. It is the second largest country in Europe, after Russia, and almost the entire country is one vast plain of extremely fertile black soils. Once known as the bread basket of the USSR, the Ukraine has a rich tradition of bread making. Emigré bakers in Britain and America, as well as European bread specialists, produce some excellent breads. A popular Ukrainian loaf is a sourdough bread made with a half rye, half wheat flour blend. It is baked on the sole of the oven and has a good chewy crust and a noticeably sour flavour.

HUNGARIAN SPLIT FARMHOUSE LOAF

*450g/1lb/4 cups unbleached white
bread flour
10ml/2 tsp salt
2.5ml/½ tsp fennel seeds, crushed
15ml/1 tbsp caster sugar
20g/¾ oz fresh yeast
275ml/9fl oz/1⅛ cups lukewarm water
25g/1oz/2 tbsp butter, melted*

*For the Topping
1 egg white
pinch of salt
10ml/2 tsp fennel seeds, for sprinkling*

Makes 1 Loaf

*A golden, fennel seed-encrusted loaf with a moist white crumb. It is equally
delicious made into rolls – just reduce the baking time to 15–20 minutes.*

1 Lightly grease a baking sheet. Sift the white bread flour and salt together into a large bowl and stir in the crushed fennel seeds and caster sugar. Make a well in the centre.

2 Cream the yeast with a little water, stir in the rest, then pour into the centre of the flour. Stir in sufficient flour to make a runny batter. Sprinkle more of the flour on top, cover and leave in a warm place for 30 minutes, or until the sponge starts to bubble and rise.

3 Add the melted butter and gradually mix in with the remaining flour to form a dough. Turn out on to a lightly floured surface and knead for 8–10 minutes until smooth and elastic. Place in a lightly oiled bowl, cover with lightly oiled clear film and leave to rise, in a warm place, for 45–60 minutes, or until doubled in bulk.

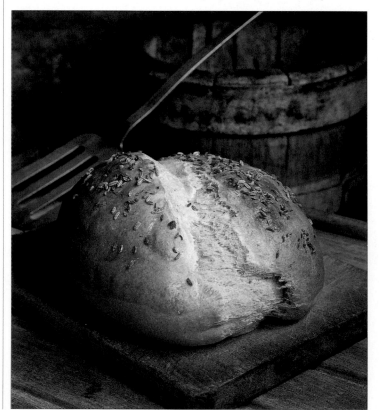

4 Turn out on to a lightly floured surface and knock back. Shape into an oval and place on the prepared baking sheet. Cover with lightly oiled clear film and leave to rise, in a warm place, for 30–40 minutes, or until doubled in size.

5 Meanwhile, preheat the oven to 220°C/ 425°F/Gas 7. Mix the egg white and salt together, and brush this glaze over the loaf. Sprinkle with fennel seeds and then, using a sharp knife, slash along its length. Bake for 20 minutes, then reduce the oven temperature to 180°C/ 350°F/Gas 4 and bake for 10 minutes more, or until sounding hollow when tapped on the base. Transfer to a wire rack to cool.

GEORGIAN KHACHAPURI

These savoury buns are sold from street stalls as warm snacks. The sealed bread parcels envelop a meltingly delicious cheese filling; goat's cheese is typically used in Georgia.

225g/8oz/2 cups unbleached white
bread flour
5ml/1 tsp salt
15g/½ oz fresh yeast
150ml/¼ pint/⅔ cup lukewarm milk
25g/1oz/2 tbsp butter, softened

FOR THE FILLING
225g/8oz/2 cups grated mature
Cheddar cheese
225g/8oz Munster or Taleggio cheese,
cut into small cubes
1 egg, lightly beaten
15ml/1 tbsp butter, softened
salt and freshly ground black pepper

FOR THE GLAZE
1 egg yolk
15ml/1 tbsp water

MAKES 4 BUNS

3 Turn the dough out onto a lightly floured surface and knead for 2–3 minutes. Divide into 4 equal pieces and roll each out into a 20cm/8in circle.

4 Place one dough circle in one hole of the Yorkshire pudding tin and fill with a quarter of the cheese filling. Gather the overhanging dough into the centre and twist to form a topknot. Repeat with the remaining dough and filling. Cover with lightly oiled clear film and leave to rise, in a warm place, for 20–30 minutes.

1 Lightly grease a Yorkshire pudding tin with four 10cm/4in holes. Sift the flour and salt into a large bowl. Cream the yeast with the milk, add to the flour and mix to a dough. Knead in the butter, then knead on a lightly floured surface until smooth and elastic. Place in a lightly oiled bowl, cover with lightly oiled clear film and leave to rise, in a warm place, for 1–1½ hours, or until doubled in bulk.

2 Meanwhile, put the cheeses in a bowl and stir in the egg and softened butter for the filling. Season with plenty of salt and pepper.

VARIATIONS
• Use Red Leicester or Parmesan in place of the Cheddar.
• Make one large bread instead of the buns. Bake for 50–55 minutes.

5 Meanwhile, preheat the oven to 180°C/350°F/Gas 4. Mix the egg yolk and water, and brush over the dough. Bake for 25–30 minutes, or until light golden. Cool for 2–3 minutes in the tin, then turn out on to a wire rack. Serve warm.

THE BREADS OF GREECE, CYPRUS AND TURKEY

Greece has a wonderful array of breads, arising from historical and geographical influences. Here, not only are there the Arabian-style breads of the Ottoman Empire, but also indigenous breads with a long history, which are still baked, particularly on the islands, by people who keep these traditions alive. On some of the Aegean Islands, up until very recently, the wheat and barley harvested by smallholders would be carried to the windmill for milling into flour. The dough would then be made and shaped, before being taken to the village oven for baking. Such traditions have now almost entirely died out, and in the cities the bakeries are as sophisticated as those anywhere else in Europe. But in many small villages, on the islands or in the mountains, people still buy the simple but large white crusty bread, which is frequently still baked in an old brick oven, the brushwood being collected by the baker or his family each evening ready for the next day's baking.

Throughout Greece, local bakers produce their own particular bread, which necessarily becomes a favourite with their customers. In the cities, the more enterprising bakeries produce a wide range of breads flavoured with raisins, olives and herbs, but among the islands and in the mountains, most loaves continue to be of the plain, farmhouse variety – large and crusty and sometimes scattered with sesame seeds. The bread has a slightly coarse texture, which makes it excellent for mopping up sauces and dressings.

Travelling eastwards from Greece, the leavened breads of Europe give way to the characteristic flat breads of the Middle East. However, inevitably there are breads that are common to Greece and Turkey, partly because of the crossover of ideas and partly because some breads, such as pitta, are so versatile that their popularity endures.

BREADSTICKS

Although similar to Italian *grissini*, Greek and Turkish breadsticks are somewhat chunkier, although just as crunchy. They are mostly sprinkled with sesame or poppy seeds, or may be made using fennel, which gives them a noticeable aniseed flavour. *Koulouria* are similar but the bread has been formed into rings, like pretzels. Sold by itinerant street vendors from their large wicker baskets, these too are often liberally sprinkled with sesame seeds, in which case they are referred to as *thessalonikis*.

PAN BREAD

You are only likely to come across this bread, called *tiganópsoma* in Greek, if you visit the delightful Greek island of Santorini, believed by some to be the site of the lost world of Atlantis. It is a simple unleavened bread, mixed to a thick batter and combined with onions and tomatoes before being fried.

GREEK CELEBRATION BREADS

Bread has religious significance all over the world, but nowhere more so than in Greece. Almost all of the important days in the religious calendar have their own speciality bread – some rich with fruit, eggs and butter, others completely plain, depending on the holy day that is being celebrated.

Prosforo (holy bread) is the bread of the Greek Mass, prepared by bakers every Saturday and taken to the church on Sunday by a member of the congregation. The large, round white loaf is stamped with the church seal and is the Host of the Communion, shared out by the priest to the faithful during the Mass.

LEFT: Breadsticks

RIGHT: Daktyla is a popular Greek bread.

On Clean Monday, which is the first day of Lent in the Greek Orthodox Church, the *lagana* is the centre-piece of a traditional meal of seafood and salads. Clean Monday is so-called since on this day Greek housewives are expected to scrub the kitchens and all utensils, to make sure nothing remains of Celebration – the three-week long festival that precedes the fasting of Lent. Appropriately, the *lagana* is a completely plain unleavened bread, made by local bakers solely for this one day of the year. The dough is formed into a large oval and then sprinkled with sesame seeds before baking.

Tsoureki is the famous Greek Easter bread. The yeasted bread is made from an enriched dough flavoured with orange and spices. It can be coiled into a round, but is more frequently made into a long plait and then scattered with almonds and sesame or caraway seeds and decorated with the characteristic red hard-boiled eggs. If you visit Greece just before Easter, you will find packets of red-dyed eggs sold everywhere. They symbolize the Resurrection and are knocked together after the Midnight Mass on Easter Saturday evening with the words, "Christ is Risen". On many of the Greek islands, where old customs still continue, *tsoureki* is the traditional Easter gift from children to their godparents.

Another festive and enriched bread is the *christopsomo*, the Greek Christmas bread. The top is decorated with a large cross, fashioned from the dough, the ends of which encircle cherries or walnuts.

OLIVE BREAD (ELIOTI)

Originally this bread was a Lenten food for the priests of the Eastern Orthodox Church, although now *elioti* is produced all over the country and can be enjoyed at any time of the year. It is generally a white bread, enriched with a little olive oil, flavoured with marjoram or oregano and studded with black olives.

DAKTYLA

This unmistakable loaf is a style of bread that belongs equally to Greece, Cyprus and Turkey. Its defining characteristic is the liberal addition of nigella seeds in the bread itself, and the white sesame and black nigella seeds sprinkled

LEFT: There is a rich variety of white breads in Greece, often sprinkled with sesame seeds.

BELOW:
Ekmek

over the top. The bread is oval and is normally large. It has deep slashes along the crust and looks like a large bloomer. It has a slightly peppery flavour thanks to the nigella seeds, and an open, coarse texture.

CILICIAN BREAD

Available now in many countries, these small flat breads sprinkled with cheese and spices are like miniature pizzas.

PITTA (PIDE)

Pitta breads, or *pide* to give them their Turkish name, are probably the best-known Greek and Turkish breads. This style of bread – flat and baked so that it contains a pocket – is found all over the Middle East, although often in different shapes and known by different names. Although pitta is a flat bread, it is not an unleavened bread. There is little crumb but the crust is soft and it is leavened with yeast; the flatness and characteristic pocket, called the *mutbag*, are due to the method of baking – ideally in an extremely hot clay oven. Pitta breads are widely eaten outside of Greece and Turkey, used as they are intended for stuffing with meats and vegetables. In restaurants in Istanbul, *pide* are served straight from the oven, stuffed with chunks of lamb that has been cooked over hot embers on a nearby spit, and with yogurt and mint. There is a huge range of different pitta breads available, for example wholemeal pittas, round mini pittas, pittas flavoured with herbs or sprinkled with sesame seeds. They are best eaten warm and, when shop-bought, should be sprinkled with a little water and then placed in a hot oven or under the grill until they begin to puff up.

EKMEK

This is a large round or oval leavened bread, often dimpled like an Italian focaccia and made simply with a plain white dough. Like pitta bread, the crust is soft and is used either for stuffing for sandwiches, or using as a scoop for picking up food. *Ekmek* can also refer to other breads – the word *ekmek* simply means "bread". In Turkey you will find numerous longish loaves, sometimes made using wholemeal, but normally white flour. More elaborate *ekmeks*, baked in rounds or sprinkled with sesame seeds, can be found in bakeries in the large cities.

BELOW: Sutlu ekmek

RIGHT: Pitta bread is served almost everywhere in Greece and Turkey.

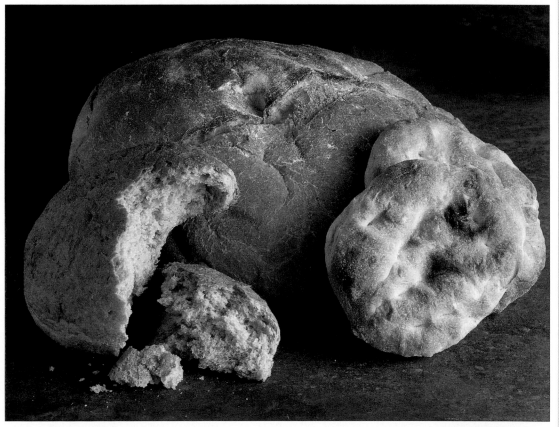

TURKESTAN BREAD

This is a proprietary loaf sold in Britain but said to be based on the bread made by Turkoman tribes who lived in the Turkestan region around the Caspian Sea.

SIMITS

These little crusty golden bread rings are sold in almost every town in Turkey, and generally first thing

ABOVE: Many Turkish bakers still use wood-burning ovens. Breads, such as pide (right) and tuzsuz (left), cook quickly with a beautifully flavoured crust and soft crumb. Hashas (centre) is a large loaf that is cooked as the oven begins to cool.

in the morning when the *simit* seller takes his wares down to the harbour and into the market to entice workers and tourists alike. *Simits* are closely related to bagels, indeed they clearly look like them, and in fact an authentic *simit* is made in the same way as a bagel, being first poached in boiling water before being sprinkled with

LEFT: Simits coated with sesame seeds.

ABOVE: Turkestan bread

sesame seeds and baked. Until quite recently, the *simit* seller would carry the rings piled high on a tray on his head or looped on to long sticks, but nowadays, food regulations mean that *simits* are more likely to be found wheeled around under glass.

GREEK OLIVE BREAD

675g/1¹/₂ lb/6 cups unbleached white
bread flour, plus extra
for dusting
10ml/2 tsp salt
25g/1oz fresh yeast
350ml/12fl oz/1¹/₂ cups lukewarm
water
75ml/5 tbsp olive oil
175g/6oz/1¹/₂ cups pitted black olives,
roughly chopped
1 red onion, finely chopped
30ml/2 tbsp chopped fresh coriander
or mint

MAKES 2 LOAVES

VARIATION
Make one large loaf and increase the
baking time by about 15 minutes.

*The flavours of the Mediterranean simply ooze from this decorative bread,
speckled with black olives, red onions and herbs.*

5 Roll out the remaining, large piece of dough to a round. Sprinkle the olives, onion and herbs evenly over the surface, then bring up the sides of the circle and gently knead together. Cut the dough in half and shape each piece into a plump oval loaf, about 20cm/8in long. Place on the prepared baking sheets.

6 Divide the reserved dough into 4 equal pieces and roll each to a long strand 60cm/24in long. Twist together and cut in half. Brush the centre of each loaf with water and place two pieces of twisted dough on top of each, tucking the ends underneath the loaves.

7 Cover with lightly oiled clear film and leave to rise, in a warm place, for about 45 minutes, or until the loaves are plump and nearly doubled in size.

8 Meanwhile, preheat the oven to 220°C/ 425°F/Gas 7. Dust the loaves lightly with flour and bake for 35–40 minutes, or until golden and sounding hollow when tapped on the base. Transfer to a wire rack to cool.

1 Lightly grease 2 baking sheets. Sift the flour and salt together into a large bowl and make a well in the centre.

2 In a jug, blend the yeast with half of the water. Add to the centre of the flour with the remaining water and the olive oil; mix to a soft dough.

3 Turn out the dough on to a lightly floured surface and knead for 8–10 minutes until smooth. Place in a lightly oiled bowl, cover with lightly oiled clear film and leave to rise, in a warm place, for 1 hour, or until doubled in bulk.

4 Turn out on to a lightly floured surface and knock back. Cut off a quarter of the dough, cover with lightly oiled clear film and set aside.

TSOUREKI

Topped with brightly coloured eggs, this plaited bread is an important part of the Greek Easter celebrations.

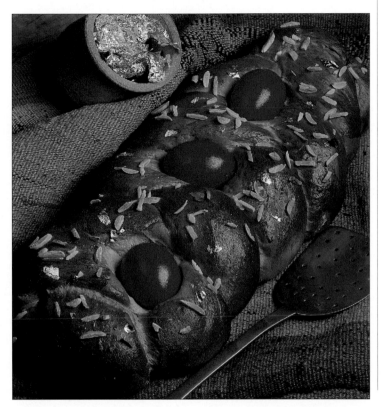

FOR THE EGGS
3 eggs
1.5ml/¼ tsp bright red food colouring paste
15ml/1 tbsp white wine vinegar
5ml/1 tsp water
5ml/1 tsp olive oil

FOR THE DOUGH
450g/1lb/4 cups unbleached white bread flour
2.5ml/½ tsp salt
5ml/1 tsp ground allspice
2.5ml/½ tsp ground cinnamon
2.5ml/½ tsp caraway seeds
20g/¾ oz fresh yeast
175ml/6fl oz/¾ cup lukewarm milk
50g/2oz/¼ cup butter
40g/1½oz/3 tbsp caster sugar
2 eggs

FOR THE GLAZE
1 egg yolk
5ml/1 tsp clear honey
5ml/1 tsp water

FOR THE DECORATION
50g/2oz/½ cup split almonds, slivered
edible gold leaf, optional

MAKES 1 LOAF

1 Lightly grease a baking sheet. Place the eggs in a pan of water and bring to the boil. Boil gently for 10 minutes. Meanwhile, mix the red food colouring, vinegar and water together in a shallow bowl. Remove the eggs from the boiling water, place on a wire rack for a few seconds to dry then roll in the colouring mixture. Return to the rack to cool and completely dry.

2 When cold, drizzle the olive oil on to absorbent kitchen paper, lift up each egg in turn and rub all over with the oiled paper.

3 To make the dough, sift the flour, salt, allspice and cinnamon into a large bowl. Stir in the caraway seeds.

4 In a jug, mix the yeast with the milk. In a bowl, cream the butter and sugar together, then beat in the eggs. Add the creamed mixture to the flour with the yeast mixture and gradually mix to a dough. Turn out the dough on to a lightly floured surface and knead until smooth and elastic.

5 Place in a lightly oiled bowl, cover with lightly oiled clear film and leave to rise, in a warm place, for about 2 hours, or until doubled in bulk.

6 Knock back the dough and knead for 2–3 minutes. Return to the bowl, re-cover and leave to rise again, in a warm place, for about 1 hour, or until doubled in bulk.

7 Knock back and turn out on to a lightly floured surface. Divide the dough into 3 equal pieces and roll each into a 38–50cm/15–20in long rope. Plait these together from the centre to the ends.

8 Place on the prepared baking sheet and push the dyed eggs into the loaf. Cover and leave to rise, in a warm place, for about 1 hour.

9 Meanwhile, preheat the oven to 190°C/375°F/Gas 5. Mix the egg yolk, honey and water together for the glaze, and brush over the loaf. Sprinkle with almonds and edible gold leaf, if using. Bake for 40–45 minutes, or until golden and sounding hollow when tapped on the base. Transfer to a wire rack to cool.

The Breads of the Middle East and North Africa

A part from in Morocco, which bestrides Arabia and western Europe, almost all the breads of this enormous region are versions of flat breads. Tradition and culture play a part here. In many of these regions people have always led a nomadic existence, living in tents and moving frequently from place to place. There was never any time nor inclination for plates or cutlery and when it came to eating, bread was used both as a food in its own right and as a means of conveying other food to the mouth. In addition, fuel was scarce and bread had to be cooked quickly while the fire was hot. Flat breads that cooked in minutes were a far better option than large, sturdy loaves. Even today, clay ovens almost identical to those depicted on walls of ancient tombs can still be found in some of the smaller villages of Egypt, Iran and Turkey. The ovens are fuelled with wood, corn kernels or even camel dung and, when they are hot, the flattened dough is baked against the sides of the walls.

Although the bread is flat, Middle Eastern bread is generally not unleavened, apart from rare exceptions, such as the

BELOW: The flat breads of the Middle East can be indistinguishable from each other. These khoubiz are very similar to the Egyptian aiysh.

Arabian crisp bread *ragayig*. The ancient Egyptians mastered the art of leavening bread and by the 12th century BC, 40 kinds of breads and pastries were available to upper-class Egyptians from their bakeries. Wheat has always been the preferred grain. It is indigenous to Turkey and the Middle East, and the first wheat to be cultivated came from this region.

Aiysh

Aiysh is the Egyptian word for "life" and these flat round loaves must be one of the oldest breads known to mankind. We know that as long ago as 1500 BC, *aiysh* was made and sold by Egyptian bakers and the same baking methods are still used today in some parts of the country. The bread is similar to pitta bread, but smaller and thicker. It should be made with wholemeal flour. This same bread is found throughout the Middle East. The shape varies and the size ranges from 15cm/6in to 30cm/12in rounds, or ovals of up to 38cm/15in. In Yemen the bread is known as *saluf*; in Jordan and Palestine as *shrak;* and as *aiysh shami* in Syria. The bread is delicious when freshly cooked, puffing up to leave a hollow centre and a soft crust.

Khoubiz (Khobz)

This bread from the Levant and Arabian peninsula, means simply "bread" in Arabian and is virtually identical to Egyptian *aiysh*. Flat and slightly leavened, it is made in rounds varying between 15cm/6in and 30cm/12in in diameter. Originally made with a finely ground wholemeal flour similar to chapati flour, it is now more often made using white flour.

Barbari

These white breads from Iran can be oval, rectangular or round in shape, varying from small breads, about 10cm/4in long, to much larger breads measuring up to 30cm/12in. All are flattish breads and the loaves are often slashed four or five times like the French *fougasse* to give a fretwork effect. They may be brushed with oil before baking, and spiced versions with cumin or caraway seeds scattered on top are sometimes to be found.

Mankoush (Mannaeesh)

Spelt in many different ways, this is the typical Lebanese version of *khoubiz*. Here the bread is rolled into 13cm/5in rounds and indented slightly in the middle so that it is concave. It is then brushed with olive oil and *za'atar*, a blend of sesame seeds,

RIGHT: Barbari are sometimes called Persian flat breads.

unleavened. Like *lavash*, this is a large flat bread, which is quite crisp and brittle when cooked. Almost certainly the most ancient of all breads, predating even *aiysh* and *khoubiz*, *ragayig* is nevertheless still eaten today, cooked in the same way as *lavash* until it is crisp and sometimes further dried in the sun. *Nane lavash* is oval-shaped with a softer texture and is a cross between *lavash* and an Indian naan.

thyme, marjoram and *sumac*, a spice made from the dried red berries of a bush native to Sicily and western Asia. This herb and spice blend has an unusual sour flavour, thanks mainly to the *sumac*.

LAVASH

Lavash is one of the largest of the Middle Eastern flat breads. It can be round or oval, is extremely thin and can be up to 60cm/2ft in diameter. The bread came originally from Armenia and Iran, although its popularity has spread and it is widely eaten all over the Middle East. The dough is often taken by villagers to the local bakery to be slowly baked in clay ovens called *furunji*. Alternatively, it is baked in a *sorj*, a dome-covered oven like an inverted

BELOW: Flat breads, such as this mankoush from the Lebanon cook quickly and are ideal in lands where fuel is scarce.

wok. Cooked in this way, the bread becomes brittle and crisp and is generally eaten straight away, torn in large pieces. *Lavash* can be unleavened or leavened, but its close relative, *ragayig*, is always

PIDEH

This is an Armenian version of the Turkish *pide*; it is always made using wholemeal flour. The rolled-out breads are scattered with sesame seeds before being baked in the oven.

MOROCCAN AND TUNISIAN BREADS

There are several types of Moroccan bread, mostly variations on the same theme. The wheat flour dough, can be white, wholemeal or a blend of both, and may be enriched with olive or peanut oil. It may be leavened naturally, although yeasts are more commonly used these days. Either way, the loaf is almost always round and flattish and equally invariably, is made by wives and daughters at home. In the past, and even now among some families, the unbaked loaves are carried to the local bakery to be cooked.

MOROCCAN HOLIDAY BREAD

Cornmeal, together with pumpkin and sunflower seeds, makes this a tasty bread. It is baked for special occasions.

TUNISIAN KESRET

This version of the Arabian bread, *khoubiz*, is mainly distinguished by the fact that it is cooked in a tagine, a North African earthenware cooking pot.

MELLA

This round flat bread, made by Tunisian nomads and sometimes containing caraway seeds, is covered with sand before being placed on the embers of a fire.

MARRAKESH SPICED BREAD

Moroccan cuisine reveals a number of cultural influences. France's short but significant domination with its invasion in the middle of the 19th century is noticeable in a number of spheres. French is still an important language in Morocco and many dishes clearly owe their inspiration to French cuisine, albeit with spicy flavours that are entirely local. Marrakesh spiced bread owes much to the French brioche – made with a yeasted white dough and enriched with butter and sometimes eggs – yet it is very much a product of Morocco. Flower water, either orange or rose, gives it a strongly perfumed taste and it is also sugary sweet, especially when served with honey or jam.

Jewish Breads

You do not have to travel far to enjoy this rich selection of breads. Wherever there is a Jewish community, a huge range of their particular breads will be produced, both for daily eating and for festivals and celebrations. The other singular aspect of Jewish breads, in contrast to English or French breads, for example, is that by definition, they do not belong to one country or region. Jewish cuisine embraces an enormous spectrum of culinary traditions, ranging across eastern and central Europe, through the Mediterranean, the Middle East, north-east Africa and India.

Visit a Jewish delicatessen and you will find a surprising number of loaves bearing a close resemblance to the breads of Germany, Russia or eastern Europe. The harmonization of ideas that occurs when people become neighbours is particularly apparent with age-old traditions such as bread making, and cultures are decidedly richer for it.

CHALLAH

There are many variations on this spectacular festive bread with its deep brown crust and soft white crumb. Challah is traditionally made for the

ABOVE: Rich challah spirals

Sabbath or for other Jewish holidays and while it is most often seen plaited, it can be shaped into spirals or wreaths, or baked in a tin. The dough is made using eggs and vegetable oil, which gives it a soft texture somewhere between that of a brioche and a soft white loaf. It is normally slightly sweetened, with either sugar or

honey; the sweeter loaves also being stuffed with raisins. The most popular *challahs*, however, are simply liberally sprinkled with poppy seeds, which is one of their most characteristic features.

In Orthodox Jewish families two loaves of *challah* are placed on the traditional embroidered tablecloth. A blessing is said over the bread, before it is broken and handed to members of the family. The Hebrew word for "blessing" is *brachah*, which derives from the Ashkenazi (eastern European) word for plaited bread. The two loaves represent the manna sent down by God to the Israelites after leaving Egypt.

Challah can be plaited with three, six or twelve strands of dough. At Rosh Hashanah, it is customary to have round *challahs*, often sweetened with honey and sometimes enriched with raisins or sultanas. On the eve of Yom Kippur, *challah* is baked in the shape of wings, a ladder or raised arms, symbolizing prayers being made to heaven.

ABOVE: A plaited challah

BOULKAS

These are small roll-sized *challahs*, shaped into rounds, plaits or spirals and made especially for weddings. However, they are often baked and sold by large bakeries for any occasion.

BAGELS

The bagel – "the roll with a hole" – is the customary bread at Bar Mitzvahs although nowadays they can be bought almost anywhere and enjoyed literally at any time of the year. Their unique feature, apart from the central hole, is that they are briefly poached in boiling water, or steamed for a minute, before being finally baked. The process means that the dough puffs up in the water but does not rise any more during baking, producing the characteristic dense texture. Even savoury-style bagels contain some sugar or malt extract, and a little is also added to the water during boiling. The bagel is then glazed with egg or egg white before being baked to give it a glossy crust and the result is a noticeably sweet-flavoured bread with a compact crumb and a chewy crust.

Bagels are almost always yeast-leavened, but beyond that there are countless variations. They can be made with egg, may contain cheese and/or butter, or may be made with just

BELOW: Boulkas

BELOW: Mixed bagels

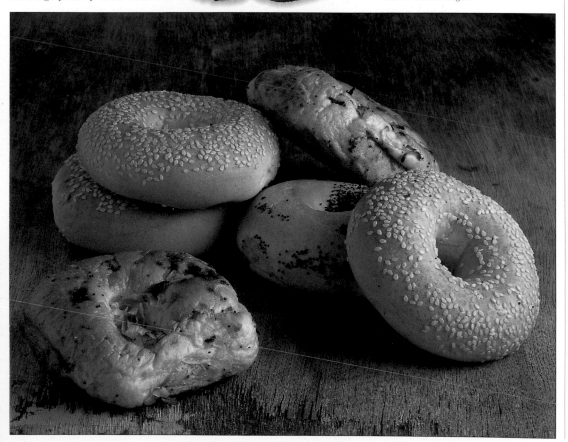

RIGHT: Shabbat bread

small, rather solid roll is basically a small dimpled bun, stuffed with fried onions. The *baily* earns its name from the city of Bailystok in Poland, which was home to many Jews before they were forced to flee due to persecution.

SUMSUMS

Sumsums are the traditional breads of the Syrian Jews and look similar to bagels, although these little rolls with a hole are not boiled before baking, but go straight into the oven after shaping. *Sumsums* are usually sprinkled with sesame seeds.

SHABBAT BREAKFAST BREAD

Known as *kubaneh*, this unique bread is always cooked overnight so it is ready for the Sabbath breakfast. The bread is from the Yemen, which has its own Jewish cuisine, and is a yeasted white dough, enriched with butter and sweetened with sugar or honey. The rolled-out dough is spread with more butter and then rolled

water and margarine. Like so many Jewish breads, the bagel seems to have originated in Europe – created, it is said, by a Polish Jew in the Middle Ages to celebrate winning a war. Centuries later, such culinary techniques were taken to New York where many Jewish immigrants settled at the turn of the 20th century. The best bagels in the world are considered to be found in New York bakeries.

Bagels are mostly eaten sliced into two flat rings. They can be plain or toasted, and are commonly spread with cream cheese, topped with lox (smoked salmon) and then eaten as a sandwich. There is, of course, no end of other fillings, kosher or not, and similarly there are countless variations. In a Jewish bakery, you are likely to find wholemeal, rye and Granary versions, along with bagels sprinkled with poppy, sesame, caraway and sunflower seeds, sea salt or chopped onion. Among the many sweet

bagels, which are widely available pre-packed in supermarkets as well as bakeries, are cinnamon and raisin-flavoured treats.

BAILYS

These are almost as popular in North America as the bagel, and both come from the same Ashkenazi Jewish culture. The

LEFT: Plain bagels

RIGHT: Matzos

JEWISH RYE BREAD

There are many varieties of Jewish rye bread, most of which originated in Eastern Europe, where rye is such a popular grain. The sourdough starter for this well-known rye is made using the crusts of previous rye breads. It is then combined with white and rye flour and caraway seeds.

MANDEL BREAD (MANDELBROT)

This is a strange kind of hybrid – part loaf, part teabread and part biscuit. The word *mandelbrot* is Yiddish for "almond bread", and the dough is fashioned into a rough loaf shape before being baked. It is not a yeasted bread but is risen using self-raising flour or baking powder and, being enriched with eggs, flavoured with lemon and vanilla and studded with almonds, it is more like a biscuit than an ordinary bread. After baking it is cut into thick diagonal slices and baked again, which transforms the loaf/teabread into chunky biscuits. Mandel breads were once extremely popular among many Jewish people throughout the world, served with wine or other drinks. However, their popularity has declined over the years and, while still baked by some Jewish bakers, they are difficult to find nowadays outside Israel and North America.

up in a spiral and then steamed in a covered baking dish in a very low oven for up to 12 hours. It can be served with sugar but is also popular Yemeni-style with spicy or garlic chutneys.

MATZO

Matzo is a piece of unleavened bread that is served in Jewish households during Passover, Feast of the Unleavened Bread. The flat, brittle bread is made and baked with great speed and under strict dietary regulations by Jewish bakers to ensure that the flour and water mixture does not start to ferment, even by accident.

Passover is the most important holiday in the Jewish calendar and celebrates the Hebrews' deliverance from slavery in Egypt. *Matzo* is a reminder of how, in their escape from the Egyptians, the Hebrews had no time to let their bread rise. Leavened bread therefore became a prohibited food during the eight days of Passover although, paradoxically, the holiday is otherwise a time of celebration and good food.

Matzo is sometimes served at the table but more commonly the bread is ground into meal and used for cakes, biscuits and dumplings during Passover (see next entry).

PASSOVER ROLLS

Since leavened bread is forbidden during Passover, Ashkenazi Jews found intriguing ways of making breads without normal flour, which even without yeast will start a natural fermentation. The trick was to use *matzos*, flat and brittle breads, that have been ground to a fine meal.

Passover rolls, which are popular among Jewish communities in Paris and other parts of Europe, are almost identical to little choux buns, made with water, butter, *matzo* meal and eggs, and baked in the oven until golden. They are normally split and filled with cream cheese or cream.

LATKES

These small potato pancakes are thought to have originated in the Ukraine, where *kartoflani placke* were a popular dish at Christmas, served with goose. The dish was apparently adopted by the large Jewish population of the area, and is now traditionally served on the feast of Chanukah.

RIGHT: Jewish or seeded rye

CHALLAH

Challah is an egg-rich, light-textured bread baked for the Jewish Sabbath and to celebrate religious holidays. It is usually plaited with 3 or 4 strands of dough, but 8 strands or more may be used to create especially festive loaves.

500g/1¼ lb/5 cups unbleached white bread flour
10ml/2 tsp salt
20g/¾ oz fresh yeast
200ml/7fl oz/scant 1 cup lukewarm water
30ml/2 tbsp caster sugar
2 eggs
75g/3oz/6 tbsp butter or margarine, melted

FOR THE GLAZE
1 egg yolk
15ml/1 tbsp water
10ml/2 tsp poppy seeds, for sprinkling

MAKES 1 LARGE LOAF

COOK'S TIP
If wished, divide the dough in half and make two small challah, keeping the plaits quite simple. Decorate with the poppy seeds or leave plain. Reduce the baking time by about 10 minutes.

1 Lightly grease a baking sheet. Sift the flour and salt together into a large bowl and make a well in the centre. Mix the yeast with the water and sugar, add to the centre of the flour with the eggs and melted butter or margarine and gradually mix in the surrounding flour to form a soft dough.

2 Turn out on to a lightly floured surface and knead for 10 minutes until smooth and elastic. Place in a lightly oiled bowl, cover with lightly oiled clear film and leave to rise, in a warm place, for 1 hour, or until doubled in bulk.

3 Knock back, re-cover and leave to rise again in a warm place for about 1 hour. Knock back, turn out on to a lightly floured surface and knead gently. Divide into 4 equal pieces. Roll each piece into a rope about 45cm/18in long. Line up next to each other. Pinch the ends together at one end.

4 Starting from the right, lift the first rope over the second and the third rope over the fourth. Take the fourth rope and place it between the first and second ropes. Repeat, starting from the right, and continue until plaited.

5 Tuck the ends under and place the loaf on the prepared baking sheet. Cover with lightly oiled clear film and leave to rise in a warm place, for about 30–45 minutes, or until doubled in size. Meanwhile, preheat the oven to 200°C/400°F/Gas 6. Beat the egg yolk and water for the glaze together.

6 Brush the egg glaze gently over the loaf. Sprinkle evenly with the poppy seeds and bake for 35–40 minutes, or until the challah is a deep golden brown. Transfer to a wire rack and leave to cool before slicing.

BAGELS

Bagels are eaten in many countries, especially where there is a Jewish community, and are very popular in the USA. They can be made from white, wholemeal or rye flour and finished with a variety of toppings, including caraway, poppy seeds, sesame seeds and onion.

350g/12oz/3 cups unbleached white
bread flour
10ml/2 tsp salt
6g/1/4 oz sachet easy-blend dried yeast
5ml/1 tsp malt extract
210ml/71/2 fl oz/scant 1 cup
lukewarm water

FOR POACHING
2.5 litres/4 pints/21/2 quarts water
15ml/1 tbsp malt extract

FOR THE TOPPING
1 egg white
10ml/2 tsp cold water
30ml/2 tbsp poppy, sesame or
caraway seeds

MAKES 10 BAGELS

5 Meanwhile, preheat the oven to 220°C/425°F/Gas 7. Place the water and malt extract for poaching in a large saucepan, bring to the boil, then reduce to a simmer. Place the bagels in the water 2 or 3 at a time and poach for about 1 minute. They will sink and then rise again when first added to the pan. Using a fish slice or large draining spoon, turn over and cook for 30 seconds. Remove and drain on a dish towel. Repeat with the remaining bagels.

1 Grease 2 baking sheets. Sift the flour and salt together into a large bowl. Stir in the dried yeast. Make a well in the centre. Mix the malt extract and water, add to the centre of the flour and mix to a dough. Knead on a floured surface until elastic.

2 Place in a lightly oiled bowl, cover with lightly oiled clear film and leave to rise, in a warm place, for about 1 hour, or until doubled in bulk.

3 Turn out on to a lightly floured surface and knock back. Knead for 1 minute, then divide into 10 equal pieces. Shape into balls, cover with clear film and leave to rest for 5 minutes.

4 Gently flatten each ball and make a hole through the centre with your thumb. Enlarge the hole slightly by turning your thumb around. Place on a floured tray; re-cover and leave in a warm place, for 10–20 minutes, or until they begin to rise.

6 Place five bagels on each prepared baking sheet, spacing them well apart. Beat the egg white with the water for the topping, brush the mixture over the top of each bagel and sprinkle with poppy, sesame or caraway seeds. Bake for 20–25 minutes, or until golden brown. Transfer to a wire rack to cool.

BREADS OF THE AMERICAS

The United States of America yields a fabulous potpourri of breads. The thousands of people from Ireland, Italy, Germany and Scandinavia who emigrated to America at the turn of the century had little to take with them save the customs and traditions they held most dear. Baking bread would have been one of the very first tasks for the wife once a home had been established and, understandably, the breads she baked were the breads of her own country – a reminder of home and perhaps a promise of a better future.

Thriving communities were gradually established. Norwegians and other Scandinavians settled in many of the North Central states, such as Wisconsin, Minnesota and Iowa; German immigrants also settled around the Great Lakes, while in New York and in other large cities along the Eastern Seaboard, Italians and Jews made their home.

Grain, of course, was no problem in this "Land of Plenty". The United States were already world producers of grain, particularly wheat, but also rye, barley and oats. German and Eastern-European rye breads, country breads from Italy and a vast range of Jewish loaves were produced by the many

RIGHT: Hamburger buns can normally be distinguished by their sesame seed topping.

bakeries that sprang up to serve their own communities. Added to this, of course, were the established American loaves, themselves versions of breads brought to the New World by the early settlers, while in the South people moving north from Mexico continued to make their customary corn breads and tortillas. If indigenous breads can be said to exist in the United States, they are the breads made by Native Americans – whose bread-making traditions were kept alive by people of American Indian descent in North and South Dakota and other central states.

ALL-AMERICAN BREADS

While some breads are mainly popular in, for example, north-eastern, southern or south-western states, certain loaves are extremely well known throughout the whole of the United States. Some of these, such as anadama bread, are best known by reputation. These loaves are sold occasionally by small bakeries as a curiosity, but they are more widely known from recipe books as the breads handed down

by generations. Other breads, however, are the standard loaves, sold in various shapes and sizes in every supermarket and convenience store. The best are, as ever, those made by craft bakeries.

As a general rule, you will find that standard American loaves – as opposed to those made by local Italian or French bakers, for example – have a more tender and softer crumb. This is because most American loaves contain fat in the form of milk and/or melted butter.

BURGER BUN

Burgers are almost an American way of life, which makes it all the more surprising that shop-bought burger buns can be sadly disappointing. While good burger buns do exist, many of the shop-bought burger buns are not dissimilar to those found outside America – white, squashy and with a smattering of sesame seeds on top. Perhaps their very blandness is considered a necessity to contrast with the beef and relishes inside, but any American burger aficionado will tell you that, on the contrary, the bun is an integral part of the eating experience. The best burger buns are made with a simple dough but, unlike the commercial supermarket variety, do not contain the emulsifiers that give the impression you are eating soft foam. The answer, as with so many breads, is to find a good baker. Italian, French and Jewish bakers are all likely to make their own versions, using the same dough as for their standard country breads and thus producing a bun with a pleasant texture and fine flavour.

GRAHAM BREAD

There is a wide variety of American wholemeal loaves, among which Graham bread is probably king – the name being synonymous with healthy eating. The bread is named after a 19th-century doctor, Rev Sylvester Graham,

RIGHT: Graham bread

who was a keen advocate of using the whole grain for milling flour, recognizing the benefits of bran in the diet. Graham flour, Graham bread and Graham crackers are all named after him, the best and most authentic flour being stoneground and coarsely milled wholemeal flour.

BASIC WHITE BREAD

This is a simple, well-flavoured tin loaf with a slightly chewy crust and a close but soft texture.

CORNELL BREAD

This light-textured wheat germ bread is mainly of historic interest since, although it is a nutritious loaf, it has less than happy antecedents and is rarely made these days. In the 1930s Cornell University pioneered a high-protein loaf, made with wheat germ, white and soya flours, sugar and milk for patients who lived in mental hospitals. Gradually, other public institutions, such as schools and hospitals, started producing the loaf. When, in the early 1940s, during World War II, meat was either rationed or extremely

expensive, people looked for a high-protein alternative and the Cornell loaf became recommended eating. The bread clearly never recovered from such damning acclaim – even the most wonderful bread is, for most, a poor substitute to meat – and for that war generation, the scarcity and poor food that the Cornell loaf represented, meant that it became deeply unfashionable. A pity really, as recipes suggest that it is not at all bad.

BROWN AND WHOLEMEAL BREAD

There are many variations of wholemeal (wholewheat) bread. Wholewheat bread is widely available, normally in a loaf shape. There are also variations of brown bread, containing a blend of wholemeal and white flour. Wheat germ may also be added – you will need to ask or read the side of the packet to be sure. Cracked wheat bread has a delicious nutty flavour and crunchy texture, and is a good, nutritious loaf. It is usually round, although short batons and loaves are also available. It is made using milk or buttermilk, together with honey, molasses or brown sugar. The most nutritious breads are made with stoneground wholemeal flour, although white flour with added wheat germ and/or cracked wheat is still a healthy alternative with a good texture

ABOVE: Basic white bread has a soft, close texture.

ABOVE: American seven-grain (top), wholewheat (round) and cracked wheat loaves

and flavour. Seven-grain bread is another healthy loaf. It contains seven grains: normally wheat, rye and corn; and then four of the following – brown rice, buckwheat, soya, oats, barley, millet, sunflower seeds, sesame seeds or flaxseed. As you might expect, it is a dense, sturdy loaf and is popular with health-food enthusiasts.

PULLMAN LOAF
This white loaf is named after the Pullman railway coach, the box shape of which is exactly that of the bread. The bread is similar to *pain de mie*, the French sandwich loaf. It is made in a rectangular tin, rather longer than a standard loaf tin, sometimes with a sliding lid so that the crust is soft on all sides. Like *pain de mie*, it is used for sandwiches and toasting and is normally white, made American-style with butter or other fat.

SWIRL BREAD
This very attractive loaf is widely available throughout the United States. It is made by using two doughs: one of white flour, the other using a wholemeal flour to which molasses is added. The doughs are rolled out after their first rising and the wholemeal rectangle is placed on top of the white one. The two are then rolled up together. When cut, each slice of bread has a swirl pattern.

BEER BREAD
Beer and butter are the ingredients that make this a most unusual bread. It comes from Georgia and is raised by

LEFT: The Pullman loaf is used for sandwiches

RIGHT: Swirl bread: molasses gives the dough an intense colour.

cheese and has a distinctive and pleasant sour flavour. As the name suggests, it is baked in a casserole. Another dill loaf, but quite unlike the dilly casserole loaf, is the sour dill rye, which is made from a blend of wheat and rye flours, and is strongly flavoured with dillweed, caraway seeds and dill pickle brine.

CHOCOLATE BREAD

Chocolate breads are well known in the USA; bakers across the land all make their own favourite. One such

using self-raising flour or baking powder. A whole can of beer is poured into the flour mixture to make a thick batter, which is then poured into a round or rectangular loaf tin in which 50g/2oz/ ¼ cup butter has been melted. Once the loaf is cooked, it is turned upside down and the butter trickles through the bread. The result is a moist and beautifully flavoured loaf.

DILL BREAD

Dill is a popular ingredient in American breads and there are several well-known dill loaves. The dilly casserole bread is a favourite among home bakers but it can sometimes be found in delicatessens and specialist shops. As well as dill, it contains cottage

ABOVE: Dill bread

LEFT: Rustic, Italian-style sun-dried tomato bread

TOMATO BREAD

With bakers from so many nationalities, it is not surprising to find loaves in the United States that are reminiscent of other breads of the world. Tomato bread may remind you of Italian or even some Greek breads, yet here the bread has been thoroughly naturalized, the pretty, pale pink colouring coming from tomato juice, which gives the bread a definite but not overpowering taste of tomato.

SUN-DRIED TOMATO BREAD

Sun-dried tomato bread is similar to tomato bread but contains pieces of sun-dried tomatoes. It has a rustic appearance. The shape is usually a free-form round, which may be slashed across the top and dusted with flour before baking. Sun-dried tomato bread is popular served with pasta or soup.

BELOW: Triticale bread

OATMEAL BREAD

For the early settlers in America, oats were one of the easier cereals to grow and oatmeal would have been used for oat-cakes, cooked over a griddle, or, if wheat was available, added in varying proportions to flour to make loaves. Since oatmeal contains no gluten, only small quantities can be used if attempting to make anything that resembles a loaf. Wheat flour and occasionally rye flour form the basis of the dough, but oatmeal adds a pleasant flavour and texture.

chocolate loaf is called *babka*. This is a Russian-style bread that has many variations and comes in all sorts of extra-ordinary shapes. The dough, which is enriched with eggs and butter, can be plain or rich with bittersweet chocolate, and it is also sometimes filled with almond paste, raisins, nuts and more roughly chopped chocolate so that the centre is moist and soft and deliciously rich.

TRITICALE BREAD

Triticale (pronounced so as to rhyme with "daily") is a grain that has been developed using

modern gene manipulation techniques and is a hybrid of rye, durum and red win-terwheat. This probably sounds more alarming than it is – farmers and agricul-turists have been cross-breeding wheat and other cereals for hundreds of years in order to improve both yields and resis-tance to disease. The triticale grain is particularly high in protein, but low in gluten. When making dough the flour is blended with at least an equal amount of wheat flour, either white or wholemeal. The bread has a sweet and nutty flavour, that is reminiscent of rye yet without its characteristic density.

BANANA BREAD

Teabreads are immensely popular throughout the USA and all sorts of fruits and vegetables are used for flavouring them. The breads are mostly made using baking powder and the mixture has more the consistency of a cake than a dough. Consequently most American teabreads are baked in tins, after which they are

OPPOSITE: Babka, a Russian-style chocolate loaf, comes in all shapes and sizes.

ABOVE: Oatmeal bread has a good texture and flavour.

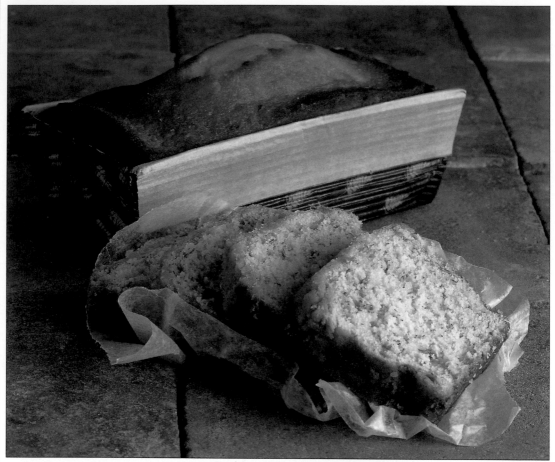

turned out and thickly sliced to serve with tea or with morning coffee. Bananas are a favourite teabread ingredient.

LEMON BREAD

Lemon bread is as popular as all the other teabreads. It is a finer flavoured and more textured loaf than most teabreads. Lemon in the form of rind or extract is often added to other teabreads, but is wonderful when given a starring role.

RIGHT: Plaited Cheddar cheese bread that is flavoured with beer.

ABOVE: Lemon bread and banana bread

CHEDDAR CHEESE BREAD

There are all sorts of flavoured breads in the United States and cheese is a favourite ingredient. Grated cheese can be kneaded into the dough to give it a rich, soft flavour, or else sprinkled on top to melt into the crust. Cheddar cheese bread is a simple but tasty yeast-leavened loaf that is almost always made with white flour. It is excellent with soups and barbecues, and is delicious toasted. A plaited cheese loaf is sometimes made using beer rather than milk or water.

NORTH-EAST AMERICAN BREADS

This is the area of the original 13 colonies, founded by the Pilgrim Fathers. The Dutch came, too, as well as other pilgrims seeking religious freedom. Among these people were the Amish, whose communities can today be found in Ohio and Indiana but most famously in Pennsylvania. New York is the epicentre of this region and here can be found a breathtaking range of breads from countries all over the world. But the most famous of all New York's bread, notwithstanding the Italian ciabattas, Irish soda breads, and baguettes and *pain de campagne* from France, are the Jewish breads. New York has the biggest community of Jews outside Israel and the city is distinguished for having the best bagels in the world. National breads can be found under their own separate heading, but the following are a selection of breads that have evolved from the recipes settlers adapted to the cereals and climate they found in the New World.

ANADAMA BREAD

The anecdote behind this bread is so good that few bread books can resist it, although it is not generally a bread found in most bakers or supermarkets. The bread dates back to colonial times and is unusual since it is one of the rare cornmeal breads made with yeast. The story goes that an irritable New England woodsman had a wife by the name of Anna, who fed him nothing but a cornmeal and molasses mush for supper. One evening, having had more than he could take, he grabbed some flour and yeast off the shelf, mixed it into the mush and put it in the oven to bake, muttering "Anna, damn her" over and over again. Thus the name, "anadama" came about. The loaf is made with yellow cornmeal and wheat flour in varying proportions and is normally baked in a round cake tin.

BOSTON BROWN BREAD

The Pilgrims who arrived in Massachusetts and other New England states must have quickly found that rye, rather than wheat, flourished better in the cold snowy winters and cool summers of their new home. This bread is one of the best known of the old breads – made with rye blended with cornmeal and white flour, which was a common practice in poorer families where corn was easily available but wheat was not. The bread is steamed – these days normally in large coffee cans, but presumably originally in ceramic pudding moulds. The advantage was that the bread could be made without the need for an oven, another sign that this was a bread of poor people, who strove to make do with the resources they had. The bread is often sweetened with molasses and/or buttermilk, which gives it a distinctive sour/sweet flavour, and is a favourite to eat with Boston baked beans.

BAKED BROWN BREAD/DUTCH OVEN BREAD

This is similar in many ways to Boston brown bread: it is made using rye flour, cornmeal and wheat flour, with molasses and buttermilk. The difference is in the baking. Unlike Boston brown bread, which is steamed, this loaf is baked in the oven. It was originally baked in a Dutch oven, a round type of pot set over a fire. Today, it is normally cooked in a covered casserole. The bread is placed in a cold oven and then baked until firm.

NEW ENGLAND BUTTERMILK ROLLS

These small, yeast and soda-risen breads are light and flaky with a delightful soft crumb, thanks to the buttermilk from which they are made.

EGG HARBOUR BREAD

The bread is made by the Amish, a Mennonite people of Swiss and Dutch origin, who fled their own countries in the 18th century due to religious persecution in Europe. They migrated first to Pennsylvania, where their descendants are called Pennsylvania Dutch, and then moved to Ohio and other Midwest states. Everything about their life and lifestyle is plain and simple. This white bread from a village on the shores of Lake Michigan is typical – a plain white yeasted dough that is allowed six risings before being baked, which gives a beautifully textured loaf with a soft crumb. Old-order Amish bread is made by the families in northern Indiana. The bread is

RIGHT: New England buttermilk rolls are light and flaky.

RIGHT: Yankee cornbread is a yellow savoury bread, sometimes made with bacon.

made from flour milled only from the hard spring wheats.

YANKEE CORN BREAD

Corn bread is normally thought of as a southern-style bread where corn is the predominant cereal grown. However, there are several corn breads made in the northern states, which differ from their southern counterparts by being far thicker and using a yellow cornmeal. The majority of northern corn breads, excepting those from New England, are fairly sweet, may be round, square or rectangular and are a pale yellow in colour rather than white. In spite of their sweetness they are savoury breads, sometimes made with bacon and usually served hot, with butter.

HOE CAKES

The first English settlers in America, the Pilgrim Fathers, had only the local cereal for bread until their own crops could be grown and harvested. Corn was by far the most common cereal cultivated by the Native Americans and must have seemed a preferable option to the uncertainty of the settlers' own wheat. Corn though was something the English had never come across before. Whether by trial and error, or with the help of the Native Americans, the colonists learnt how to grind the corn kernels to make a meal that could be made into bread. These small flat cakes were cooked over the open fire, balanced on an agricultural hoe, and hence got their name, "hoe cakes". Bacon fat was used both to grease the hoes and to add flavour to the otherwise bland breads.

Although not generally made now, hoe cakes are sometimes produced as a curiosity by restaurants in Massachusetts and New York State that wish to recapture aspects of 17th-century life.

ABOVE: Old-order Amish bread is also known as North American spring loaf. The long fermentation period means it has an excellent flavour.

MIDWEST AND NORTH CENTRAL AMERICAN BREADS

These are the heartlands of America, stretching from the dairy farms of Wisconsin to the prairies of Wyoming. Here in middle America, great store is set by family life with family meals being a central part. These states were settled mainly by Scandinavians, Germans and Slavs who brought with them the traditions of their homeland. Sourdough ryes and mixed-grain loaves are therefore among the most common breads available.

SALT-RISING BREAD

There are several recipes in American cookbooks for salt-rising breads, but it is thought that the bread was originally made by pioneers crossing the Midwest and western prairies. The starter dough would have been carried in crocks, as the horse- or oxen-drawn wagons made their way across the plains. "Salt-rising" refers to the practice of keeping the active starter in a bowl nestling in a bed of salt, which is easy to warm and retains its heat for a long time. The starter would provide the leaven for fresh bread, which would have been made and baked in makeshift ovens each time the wagon train stopped.

BELOW: Seeded rye (left) and old Milwaukee rye

Although an authentic bread of the prairies, nowadays this bread is a speciality of some of the East Coast bakers. The 19th-century sourdough loaf is known for its delicious and delicate crumb, yet also renowned for the difficulty in actually getting it to work. Several bakeries have succeeded with the bread, but the starter, made from scalded milk, sugar and cornmeal, is a notoriously tricky one to prepare. Once the starter begins to ferment, milk, white flour, fat, sugar and salt are added to make a sponge. This adds another potential complication as salt is never usually added to a starter or sponge because it tends to inhibit the yeast. Given the right conditions of warmth and humidity, however, the sponge should rise and fall, after which the remaining flour is added and the dough made into bread in the usual fashion.

LEFT: Heavy sour rye bread

RYE BREAD

There are many rye breads in the Midwest states of Wisconsin, Ohio, Minnesota, Iowa and Nebraska. Pumpernickel is commonly sold, as is a crusty rye bread made using rye and wheat flour but often with butter added, which is a feature of many American breads. Like most traditional ryes, Old Milwaukee rye is a sourdough loaf, made with molasses and flavoured in typical Germanic-style with caraway seeds. The bread may be shaped into round loaves or fashioned into long, slender ones.

SEEDED RYE

Seeded rye bread is often known as Jewish rye and is popular not only in the Midwest, but as far east as New York.

ABOVE: Salt-rising bread

HEAVY SOUR RYE BREAD

This is known as "corn bread" from the cornmeal that is sprinkled on the baking sheet, but is otherwise a rye sourdough made with a proportion of wheat flour. It is normally liberally sprinkled with caraway seeds. The bread is frequently sold by weight and can be recognized by its sides, which are liberally sprinkled with cornmeal, and its top, which is scattered with caraway seeds.

WEST COAST AMERICAN BREADS

In California, fashions come and go so quickly that it is surprising to find that some of the most traditional American breads are not only still being produced but are ever more popular – in the delicatessens, the restaurants and on the dinner party circuit. Many influences have come to play a part. The Pacific Coast was the end of the journey for pioneers hoping to find opportunity and freedom: Hispanics, from the south, gravitated towards the cities of Los Angeles and San Francisco, while Europeans settled all over the region, each culture establishing its own favourite styles of cooking and enthusiastically sampling others.

SAN FRANCISCAN SOURDOUGH

San Franciscan sourdough is probably the best-known American bread outside the United States, and is one that can be truly said to be all-American. It is a round, wheat, oven-baked loaf, with a star slash or a cross-hatched pattern on top. These breads, like the salt-rising breads, were brought to the West Coast by pioneers who crossed the prairies and plains of middle America in search of gold. The trip took the early pioneers five or six months and was extremely hazardous. The Forty-Niners – the men who took part in the 1849 Gold Rush – gave their camps names like Hell's Half Acre and Hangtown, which gives an idea of what life must have been like. Provisions for the journey included sacks of flour, together with a small piece of leavening kept back from the last batch of dough, so that bread could be baked en route. The leavening was stored in a crock inside a sack of flour.

The word "sourdough" refers quite simply to the bread's flavour. The bread has the same sharp/sour taste of yogurt or buttermilk.

It is said that it is impossible to make San Franciscan sourdough outside the city itself. The climate of San Francisco, with

LEFT: Perhaps America's best-known bread, the San Franciscan sourdough.

its warmth and humidity, is particularly conducive to sourdough breads, and the bacterium, which feeds on the flour and water mixture, is unique to that area. However, home-bakers often attempt approximations, while professional bakeries all over California produce their own versions, including the *Berkeley sourdough*, which is a baguette-shaped loaf.

MONKEY BREAD

This bread goes under a variety of names, including bubble loaf or poppy seed bubble loaf. The bread normally comprises seven or eight small dough balls baked in a ring mould so that when it is baked the bread does look like lots of bubbles. The little balls are dipped into melted butter and then sprinkled with poppy seeds or currants, raisins, nuts and/or sugar and cinnamon before being baked.

SOUTH-WEST AMERICAN BREADS

Texas, New Mexico and Arizona all border Mexico and their cuisine, including the bread, shows all the influences of its southern neighbour. Food can be spicy and very hot, and tortillas and other corn breads are as common as breads made with wheat.

JALAPEÑO CORN BREAD

This is a typical Tex-Mex-style bread, made with a blend of cornmeal and white flour. Hot jalapeño chillies are kneaded into the dough, and some loaves may contain whole corn kernels and cheese, too. The bread can be baked in loaf tins or shaped into rounds and oven bottom-baked and it has a unique, snappy flavour.

SOPAIPILLAS

These small, puffy breads are a speciality of New Mexico. They are made by mixing together flour, baking powder and salt, adding water to make a dough and then incorporating some vegetable fat, as when making puff pastry. The dough is then rolled out extremely thinly and cut into small squares, which are deep fried until puffy. If made professionally in a restaurant or by a baker, the corners can then be snipped off and filled with honey. Otherwise honey or syrup can simply be poured over the breads. A savoury alternative uses refried beans.

HOBO BREAD

Hobo bread is so-called, not because it is a favourite among tramps and vagrants, but because it is traditionally eaten outdoors. It is a sweet bread, rich with sultanas and nuts, that has been baked in a coffee can so that it is shaped like a long cylinder. Its popularity as an outdoor bread is probably due to the fact that the bread keeps well for several months. It is normally stored in the can in which it is cooked.

BREADS OF THE SOUTHERN STATES

This region includes Mississippi, Alabama and Georgia among others. Corn is cultivated in many of these states and the popularity of corn breads is well known, many people preferring the flat and rather mealy flavour of the corn to the wheat breads popular in the north.

NEW ORLEANS BREAD

New Orléans has many visible French influences – including its name, after Orléans in France – and not least its excellent breads *Pain perdu* (French toast) is a favourite breakfast for many New Orléans citizens. New Orléans' French bread is softer than the real French version. It is sometimes known as feather bread and is very light. It has the same open texture as the French baguette, but has added fat and sugar, which makes it slightly richer and sweeter.

SPOON BREAD

This corn confection is part bread, part dessert, known as spoon bread for the simple reason that it has to be eaten with a spoon. It is the consistency of custard and is puffy and creamy when cooked. It is then liberally doused in corn syrup or honey and is very sweet. The bread is made with cornmeal, a little white flour, eggs, milk and baking powder. One story suggests that the bread was created when too much liquid was added to a corn bread batter and the baked bread had to be spooned out of the tin. Be that as it may, the Virginians insist that this event happened in one of their kitchens and thus claim spoon bread as their own. In Virginia, you will find this served both as a dessert and as a savoury course, made with bacon, cheese and garlic.

SOUTHERN CORN BREAD

There are numerous corn breads in the southern states. Convenience stores and supermarkets sell the more standard-type loaves, but in the home people still make their own breads, and since corn bread is best eaten as soon as possible, these are going to be the most tasty. Corn breads only rarely use yeast, and are relatively quick and easy to make. Southerners like white cornmeal for their breads, rather than the yellow meal preferred in the north and the breads are generally much thinner. Wheat flour is added to these breads in varying proportions, but in southern corn bread neither wheat flour nor fat is added, so that the corn flavour is predominant.

Other breads, such as rich corn bread, are made using cream, milk, butter and eggs. Corn pone is thought to be directly inspired by the Native Americans. It is a small, moist loaf, which is made from finely ground cornmeal along with buttermilk and lard.

NATIVE AMERICAN FRY-BREAD

People have lived in America for thousands of years, developing into various local populations of Native Americans who made bread from both wheat and corn for special occasions and for everyday eating. Hoe cakes made by early English settlers may well be adaptations or even pure copies of the breads made by the local people. Nowadays, there are reservations for Native Americans in various American states such as Oklahoma, and several of the more northern states. Their breads vary a little in size but are surprisingly similar across the continent, being small flat breads made from a flour and water dough that is rolled thinly and cut into diamonds, circles or squares. In North and South Dakota on the Sioux reservation, the breads are called "fry-breads" and are made for powwows – ceremonies or inter-tribal gatherings featuring much feasting and dancing.

SALLY LUNN

This famous bread from Bath in England is said to have been brought to America by the English settlers. It is well known all over the United States but has become a popular speciality bread in the South, where it is served for lunch or tea. The American version was originally made in a Turk's-head mould, but is now less elaborate, baked in a tube tin. There are also miniature versions baked in *petit four* tins, and muffin-size versions made in muffin tins.

CRANBERRY NUT BREAD

This loaf is a bread enriched with eggs and butter, and is famous for the bright red berries that speckle the loaf. Cranberries are in season during November which is why the bread is often associated with Thanksgiving and Christmas. Cranberry nut bread is commonly given as a gift at this time and is popular for its tart taste, which is often accentuated with the flavour of orange.

ZUCCHINI BREAD

Courgettes, or zucchini as they are known in the USA, are hugely popular, not only as a side vegetable, but for use in cakes, muffins and bread. The sweet bread, made with coarsely grated courgettes, sweet spices and sugar, and enriched with eggs and oil, can be iced or served as a dessert cake.

ABOVE: Southern corn bread is made from white cornmeal.

MONKEY BREAD

This American favourite is also called bubble bread – because of the "bubbles" of dough. The pieces of dough are tossed in a heavenly coating of butter, nuts, cinnamon and rum-soaked fruit.

7g/¼ oz sachet easy-blend dried yeast
450g/1lb/4 cups unbleached white bread flour
2.5ml/½ tsp salt
15ml/1 tbsp caster sugar
120ml/4fl oz/½ cup lukewarm milk
120ml/4fl oz/½ cup lukewarm water
1 egg, lightly beaten

FOR THE COATING
75g/3oz/½ cup sultanas
45ml/3 tbsp rum or brandy
115g/4oz/1 cup walnuts, finely chopped
10ml/2 tsp ground cinnamon
115g/4oz/⅔ cup soft light brown sugar
50g/2oz/¼ cup butter, melted

MAKES 1 LOAF

1 Lightly grease a 23cm/9in spring-form ring cake tin. Mix the dried yeast, flour, salt and caster sugar together in a large bowl and make a well in the centre.

2 Add the milk, water and egg to the centre of the flour and mix together to a soft dough. Turn out on to a lightly floured surface and knead for about 10 minutes until smooth and elastic. Place in a lightly oiled bowl, cover with lightly oiled clear film and leave to rise, in a warm place, for 45–60 minutes, or until doubled in bulk.

3 Place the sultanas in a small saucepan, pour over the rum or brandy and heat for 1–2 minutes, or until warm. Take care not to overheat. Remove from the heat and set aside. Mix the walnuts, cinnamon and sugar in a small bowl.

4 Turn out the dough on to a lightly floured surface and knead gently. Divide into 30 equal pieces and shape into small balls. Dip the balls, one at a time into the melted butter, then roll them in the walnut mixture. Place half in the prepared tin, spaced slightly apart. Sprinkle over all the soaked sultanas.

VARIATION

Replace the easy-blend dried yeast with 20g/¾ oz fresh yeast. Mix with the liquid until creamy before adding to the flour.

5 Top with the remaining dough balls, dipping and coating as before. Sprinkle over any remaining walnut mixture and melted butter. Cover with lightly oiled clear film or slide the tin into a lightly oiled large polythene bag and leave to rise, in a warm place, for about 45 minutes, or until the dough reaches the top of the tin.

6 Meanwhile, preheat the oven to 190°C/375°F/Gas 5. Bake for 35–40 minutes, or until well risen and golden. Turn out on to a wire rack to cool.

ANADAMA BREAD

A traditional bread from Massachusetts, made with molasses, cornmeal, wholemeal and unbleached white flour. According to legend, it was created by the husband of a woman called Anna, who had left a cornmeal mush and some molasses in the kitchen. On finding only these ingredients for supper her husband mixed them with some flour, water and yeast to make this bread, while muttering "Anna, damn her"!

40g/1¹/₂ oz/3 tbsp butter
120ml/4fl oz/¹/₂ cup molasses
560ml/scant 1 pint/scant 2¹/₂ cups water
50g/2oz/¹/₂ cup cornmeal
10ml/2 tsp salt
25g/1oz fresh yeast
30ml/2 tbsp lukewarm water
275g/10oz/2¹/₂ cups wholemeal flour
450g/1lb/4 cups unbleached white bread flour

MAKES 2 LOAVES

1 Grease two 1.5 litre/2¹/₂ pint/6 cup loaf tins. Heat the butter, molasses and measured water in a pan until the butter has melted. Stir in the cornmeal and salt and stir over a low heat until boiling. Cool until lukewarm.

2 In a small bowl, cream the yeast with the lukewarm water, then set aside for 5 minutes.

3 Mix the cornmeal mixture and yeast mixture together in a large bowl. Fold in the wholemeal flour and then the unbleached white bread flour to form a sticky dough. Turn out on to a lightly floured surface and knead for 10–15 minutes until the dough is smooth and elastic. Add a little more flour if needed.

4 Place in a lightly oiled bowl, cover with lightly oiled clear film and leave to rise, in a warm place, for about 1 hour, or until doubled in bulk.

VARIATION
Use a 7g/¹/₄ oz sachet easy-blend dried yeast instead of fresh. Mix it with the wholemeal flour. Add to the cornmeal mixture, then add the lukewarm water, which would conventionally be blended with the fresh yeast.

5 Knead the dough lightly on a well floured surface, shape into 2 loaves and place in the prepared tins. Cover with lightly oiled clear film and leave to rise, in a warm place, for about 35–45 minutes, or until doubled in size and the dough reaches the top of the tins.

6 Meanwhile, preheat the oven to 200°C/400°F/Gas 6. Using a sharp knife, slash the tops of the loaves 3–4 times. Bake for 15 minutes, then reduce the oven temperature to 180°C/350°F/Gas 4 and bake for a further 35–40 minutes, or until sounding hollow when tapped on the base. Turn out on to a wire rack to cool slightly. Serve warm.

CARIBBEAN AND MEXICAN BREADS

HARD-DOUGH BREAD

This fairly heavy tin or plaited white loaf is almost the standard Caribbean bread. It is the most popular bread for the islanders and is becoming increasingly popular in those parts of Britain or the United States with a sizeable Afro-Caribbean population. It has a dense, chewy texture and, like many West Indian breads, has a distinctly sweet flavour.

JOHNNY CAKES

Johnny cakes do not seem to have a single origin. There are recipes for them in a number of cookbooks from the USA as well as those from the Caribbean. Most agree however that the word is a corruption of "journey cake" – a bread that can be packed up and given to travellers for their day's journey. In Jamaica, in corroboration of this, johnny cakes can be bought freshly made from roadside stalls all over the island. Just as there is apparently no definitive ancestry, there is equally no single recipe for johnny cakes. Recipes suggest they can be made from cornmeal, wheat flour or a mixture of both. Some contain eggs and milk, while

ABOVE: Johnny cakes are a famous Jamaican bread.

the Jamaican johnny cake is made with butter or lard and coconut oil. Here the dough is shaped into balls and fried in oil. Other johnny cakes have a batter-like consistency. Cooked on a griddle or in a pan, they are served as a flat bread.

BULLA BUNS

These are spicy, round discs. They resemble muffins in appearance but are dense, dark and spicy, flavoured with allspice and rich with raisins and molasses.

CARIBBEAN BUN

A spicy teabread, this is liberally flavoured with allspice and is packed with fruit. The round buns are dark in colour and look sticky, thanks to the molasses which gives them an intense bitter/sweet flavour. Beyond the Caribbean, the buns are often available from ethnic markets and shops in larger cities and come either in small bun sizes or as a larger loaf.

TORTILLAS

Although other wheat loaves are available, tortillas are rightly known as the bread of Mexico. Freshly made and still warm, these flat breads are an essential part of every Mexican meal. Tortillas are

ABOVE: Hard-dough bread

also used in an enormous number of Mexican dishes, wrapped round meat, fish, vegetables or cheese and eaten for street food as well as snacks, suppers and elegant dinners.

There are basically two types of tortilla. Maize tortillas are made using a type of cornmeal called *masa harina*, literally meaning dough flour. These are the older of the two, having been made and eaten by native people for literally thousands of years. Until the arrival of the Spanish in the 16th century, there was no wheat in Mexico, but in northern parts of the country, where wheat flourished, wheat flour (called just flour) became the preferred choice for tortillas.

HAWAIIAN BREADS

In this delightful tropical paradise, there is a fabulous amalgamation of cultures and cuisines: along with the indigenous Hawaiians, there are Chinese, Japanese, Portuguese and people of Filipino origin.

HAWAIIAN BREAD

This is a perfect tropical bread, made with fresh coconut and macadamia nuts, which give it a ·delicious crunchy texture. The yeast-leavened white dough is enriched with eggs, butter and milk.

PORTUGUESE SWEET BREAD

Towards the end of the last century, Portuguese immigrants came to Hawaii to work in the sugar fields. Over the years their bread has acquired a character that is part Portuguese and part Hawaiian. The dough is usually yeast-leavened and enriched with eggs and butter. It is also made with condensed rather than fresh milk since the latter was once a scarce commodity on an island given over entirely to fields of sugar cane. Currants and raisins also go into the doughs, as well as being used for decoration. It may be baked in a round in a coil, but is more usually plaited and sprinkled with coarse granulated sugar.

BELOW: Bulla buns

BREAD OF THE DEAD

Should you visit Mexico around the 2 November, All Souls' Day, you may find this famous and traditional bread, called *Pan de Muerto.* It is made as part of the celebrations in memory of the deceased but, paradoxically, it is not a sad day but a fiesta. Everyone visits their relatives' graves, bringing a picnic, wearing bright colourful clothes and carrying candies and flowers along with the special bread. The bread itself comes in various forms but most often seems to be a white, yeast-risen dough, flavoured with orange and sometimes with spices. It can be a simple round or a plaited loaf coiled into a circle. The bread is then decorated with pieces of dough formed into teardrops, bones or bunches of flowers.

ABOVE: Tortillas

WEST INDIAN ROTIS

West Indian *rotis* are huge and used, as they would be in India, for mopping up stews and curries, such as curried goat. Like Indian *rotis*, they are made with chapati flour, a very fine wholemeal flour, and are cooked on a griddle. *Rotis* are best eaten warm and if you do find them in Caribbean shops, they should be sprinkled with a little water, then heated in a hot oven.

ABOVE: Spicy Caribbean bun

INDIAN BREADS

There are principally two types of Indian bread, although all share the characteristic of being flat and oval or round. In Punjab and Kashmir in the north-west and in Pakistan, Afghanistan and Bangladesh there are the naan-style breads. Their defining feature is that naans, unlike the *chapatis* and *parathas* of the south, are leavened and when cooked become light and puffy, unlike the southern breads that are unleavened and much flatter.

The north Indian breads have much in common with many of the Middle Eastern breads – they are large and flat and used as a vehicle for other foods. Recipes for naans and many breads from Syria, Egypt, Iraq and Iran are almost interchangeable. The main difference is the way in which the breads are baked.

BHAKRIS

Bhakris are flat unleavened breads made from *jowar* flour, and sometimes known as *jowar rotis*. *Jowar* is widely grown in central and southern India. The tiny green seeds from the plant can be roasted and eaten as they are, or can be milled into flour. The dough is moulded and patted flat by hand and then baked on a griddle. *Bhakris* can be plain or baked with sesame seeds, and are served with butter as a snack.

CHAPATIS

Also unleavened, chapatis are now widely known throughout Britain thanks to the popularity of Indian food. While once a more exotic request from a restaurant menu, chapatis are now almost commonplace, although the commercially available product is a rather poor imitation of the real thing. In India the chapati is popular in central and southern parts of the country, served with meals and used with the fingers to scoop up food and sauces. These authentic chapatis are made with *atta* (chapati flour), which is a very fine wholemeal flour.

ROTLAS

There are many variations of chapatis, called *rotlas*, *rotis,* and *dana rotis* to name but a few. They are all unleavened breads, made using wholemeal flour, to which ghee, oil, celery seeds and/or fresh coriander might be added. They are rolled out until thin and cooked like chapatis.

PARATHAS

Parathas are a richer and flakier version of chapatis. The chapati dough is spread with ghee, folded and then cooked over a *tava* (griddle) until puffy.

POORIS (PURIS)

These are puffier still and are available (and worth eating) only from a restaurant or by making them yourself, since they need to be eaten as soon as possible after cooking. They are normally made using a chapati dough. Small balls of dough are rolled out into 2.5cm/1in rounds and deep fried on both sides.

NAAN

The naan, unlike the chapatis of the south, is a leavened bread. The leaven varies from region to region and probably from home to home, according to the cook's preferred method. Yeast or a sourdough method can be used; others prefer using a chemical raising agent, such as bicarbonate of soda or self-raising flour. Yogurt, however, is the main ingredient that differentiates naans from its many Middle Eastern counterparts. It plays a part in fermenting the dough and some naan are made entirely using a yogurt fermentation. It is this fermentation that gives the bread its characteristic light and puffy texture and soft crust. The flavour comes

BELOW: Parathas are cooked with ghee and therefore have a golden appearance. Chapatis are cooked without any fat or oil and are thus flatter. They do not have the golden crust.

LEFT: Poppadoms are popular everywhere with Indian food.

teardrop shape. As the dough bakes, it scorches and puffs up to give a bread that is both crisp and soft in parts.

GOAN BATCH BREAD

In Goa, until recently part of Portuguese India, there is a white loaf called *pio*, possibly a corruption of *pao*, the Portuguese word for bread.

POPPADOMS

These thin crisp discs are widely available outside India, either ready-cooked or ready-to-cook. In India they are commonly served with vegetarian meals. Poppadoms are sold in markets and by street vendors: plain or flavoured with spices or seasoned with black or red pepper. The dough is generally made from dried pulses, but can also be made from potatoes or sago. It is then rolled thinly and left to dry in the sun. Poppadoms can be cooked by either deep frying or placing under a hot grill. Either way they brown in seconds and need close attention while cooking.

partly from the soured yogurt and partly, without doubt, from the *tandoor*, in which breads are traditionally cooked. A *tandoor* is a clay oven sunk into the ground and the flattened dough is baked against the blisteringly hot walls of the oven. The pull of gravity produces the

RIGHT: Naans can be plain or stuffed.

RED LENTIL DOSAS

150g/5oz/³/4 cup long grain rice
50g/2oz/¹/4 cup red lentils
250ml/8fl oz/1 cup warm water
5ml/1 tsp salt
2.5ml/¹/2 tsp ground turmeric
2.5ml/¹/2 tsp freshly ground
black pepper
30ml/2 tbsp chopped
fresh coriander
oil, for frying and drizzling

MAKES 6 DOSAS

VARIATION
Add 60ml/4 tbsp grated coconut,
15ml/1 tbsp grated fresh root ginger
and 1 finely chopped chilli to the
batter just before cooking.

Dosas and idlis are the breads of southern India. They are very different from traditional north Indian breads as they are made from lentils or beans and rice rather than flour. Dosas are more like pancakes; they are eaten freshly cooked, often at breakfast time, with chutney.

1 Place the rice and lentils in a bowl, cover with the water and leave to soak for 8 hours.

2 Drain off the water and reserve. Place the rice and lentils in a food processor and blend until smooth. Blend in the reserved water.

3 Scrape into a bowl, cover with clear film and leave in a warm place to ferment for about 24 hours.

4 Stir in the salt, turmeric, pepper and coriander. Heat a heavy-based frying pan over a medium heat for a few minutes until hot. Smear with oil and add about 30–45ml/2–3 tbsp batter.

5 Using the rounded bottom of a soup spoon, gently spread the batter out, using a circular motion, to make a 15cm/6in diameter dosa.

6 Cook for 1¹/2–2 minutes, or until set. Drizzle a little oil over the dosa and around the edges. Turn over and cook for about 1 minute, or until golden. Keep warm in a low oven over simmering water while cooking the remaining dosas. Serve warm.

PARATHAS

These triangular-shaped breads, made from a similar dough to that used for chapatis, are enriched with layers of ghee or butter to create a wonderfully rich, flaky bread.

1 Sift the flours and salt together into a large bowl. Add the oil with sufficient water to mix to a soft dough. Turn out the dough on to a lightly floured surface and knead vigorously for 8–10 minutes until smooth.

2 Place in a lightly oiled bowl and cover with a damp dish towel. Leave to rest for 30 minutes.

3 Turn out on to a lightly floured surface. Divide the dough into 9 equal pieces. Cover 8 pieces of dough with oiled clear film. Shape the remaining piece into a ball and then flatten it. Roll into a 15cm/6in round.

4 Brush with a little of the melted ghee or clarified butter and fold in half. Brush and fold again to form a triangular shape. Repeat with the remaining dough. Stack, layered between clear film, to keep moist. Heat a griddle or heavy-based frying pan.

115g/4oz/1¼ cups unbleached plain flour
115g/4oz/1 cup wholemeal flour
2.5ml/½ tsp salt
15ml/1 tbsp vegetable oil
120–150ml/4–5fl oz/½–⅔ cup water
90–120ml/3–4fl oz/scant ½ cup melted ghee or clarified butter .

MAKES 9 PARATHAS

5 Keeping the shape, roll each piece of dough to a larger triangle, with each side measuring 15–18cm/6–7in. Brush with ghee or butter and place on the griddle or in the pan, brushed side down. Cook for about 1 minute, brush with ghee or butter and turn over. Cook for about 1 minute, or until crisp and dotted with brown speckles. Keep warm in a low oven while cooking the remaining parathas. Serve the parathas warm.

AUSTRALIAN BREADS

Australia, like other countries with large immigrant communities, has a wealth of wonderful breads whose origins lie in far-off lands, plus one bread which is indigenous to the country, the famous damper. Once baked in the bush, in the embers of campfires, damper is today a favourite "barbie" food, and is almost as popular outside Australia as it originally was in the Outback.

In recent years there has been something of a revolution in Australian cooking, with some of the world's most innovative chefs producing delicious dishes based on the fine fresh ingredients for which the country is famous. Part of this revolution has been a back-to-basics approach, with more cooks seeking to get away from bland, mass-produced meals in favour of "real" food.

This is certainly true of baked goods. There has been a move away from the handy yet often horrid "cotton wool" breads, which once stacked every supermarket bakery shelf, and a return to real bread, with texture and taste.

Australian versions of Italian breads, such as focaccia, ciabatta, olive Toscano, *casalinga* and *bassotto*, and flat, Turkish

Above: The colourful and unusual vegetable il gianfornaio

bread are becoming increasingly popular, as is the brightly coloured *il gianfornaio*, which is a mosaic of red, green, yellow and orange doughs, each flavoured with a different coloured vegetable.

Leading the revolution in Australian bread making are small wood-burning bakeries, such as New Norcia in Western Australia. New Norcia is a monastic town, some 83 miles (133km) north-east of Perth. The wood-fired oven that had produced bread for the Benedictine Monks for over a century was shut down in 1989. Four years later it was fired again, and now produces – and sells – a wide range of breads, from a simple old-fashioned white loaf to their popular zucchini (courgette) bread. The monks also bake their own focaccia, an olive bread and an olive, rosemary and sun-dried tomato bread.

The breads proved so popular that a second wood-fired bakery was opened, this time in the city of Perth. Here the range is even more extensive, and includes several sourdoughs such as raisin and walnut sourdough, San Franciscan sourdough and both a light rye and a dark rye sourdough. Their unusual fig and fennel sourdough is very popular.

Supermarkets, too, have become much more adventurous, and the range of what are loosely termed "Continental breads" includes mixed grain and rye loaves with flavourings as diverse as

RIGHT: Olive Toscano

ABOVE: Ciabatta

sunflower seed and pineapple, walnut and fruit, and herb and tomato.

Many Australians bake their own bread, whether in ovens or in bread-making machines, and the range of bread mixes available is almost as interesting as the variety of breads on sale in bakeries.

AUSTRALIAN SOURDOUGH

There are a number of sourdoughs made by craft bakers. Some are made to French recipes, using a similar recipe to that used

LEFT: Potato sourdough

for the French *pain de campagne*. Potato sourdoughs, made with a potato starter, are similar to San Franciscan sourdoughs.

OLIVE TOSCANO

Like the Italian *pane Toscano*, this is a crusty, close-textured, and slightly chewy bread, made without any salt. Olive Toscano has green olives added to the dough, which add flavour and contrast well with the salt-free crumb.

DAMPER BREAD

Damper bread is the most famous and probably the only traditional bread of Australia. Like the United States' Native

ABOVE: Bassotto

American bread, it is designed to be made in the open country – in this case, in the bush. The dough, made from wheat flour and water, and sometimes flavoured with spices, is patted into cakes and baked either on hot stones or under a pot. The name "damper" comes from the fact that the fire was damped down so that the embers were just the right heat for

RIGHT. Flat Turkish bread has become one of Australia's favourite breads.

DR ALLINSON

This bread is based on the original recipe that Dr Allinson developed in the 19th century. It is a yeast-leavened bread made of organic stoneground wholemeal flour and canola (a type of cereal) and is rolled in sesame seeds before being baked in a deep-sided loaf tin.

cooking the bread. Damper bread was also sometimes made by wrapping the dough around sticks and baking it over the fire – the same method as was used for a traditional South African bread called stick bread. The sticks are removed after cooking and the holes in the bread filled with either cheese or butter.

RIGHT. Densely textured rye bread (left) and farmer rye are generally available from bakeries in the larger Australian cities.

TURKISH BREAD

Turkish bread is one of the most popular breads in Australia, particularly in Sydney. The same as Turkish *ekmet*, it too can come in varying sizes, from small rounds to large ovals. The best breads are made according to traditional Turkish methods, and are baked in wood-burning stoves.

RYE BREAD

There are various rye breads available in the cities; farmer rye is a small dense loaf, while a lite rye has a much lighter flavour and texture with a hint of malt. *Black rye* is strictly for rye lovers, and is made to an old European recipe, using a rye sourdough starter, blended with stoneground rye and wheat flour.

LEFT. Dr Allinson bread is made from organic flour and is rolled in sesame seeds before being baked in a loaf tin.

CHINESE BREADS

While for the people of southern China rice is the staple food, in the wheat-growing region of the north, bread is eaten in lieu of rice.

French-style baked loaves and rolls are becoming increasingly popular throughout the country (especially in the cities), but the traditional breads are almost always steamed. Some *dim sum* breads are fried or baked on a griddle.

MAN TO

Man to are widely eaten throughout the north of China. The small, steaming hot buns are sold everywhere – in restaurants and teahouses, on street stalls and by itinerant sellers. They are eaten sometimes as snacks, but more commonly as the traditional accompaniment to a meal, in the same way as those in the southwest of the country eat rice. They are made from white flour, yeast and sugar and then formed into small balls and steamed in wicker baskets for about 20 minutes. *Man to* have the consistency of many of the steamed *dim sum* dumplings. They can also be added to soups and other dishes.

CHICKEN BUNS (GEE BAO)

These are little steamed buns filled with a mixture of chicken and oyster sauce, and served as *dim sum*.

SPRING ONION BREAD (CHUNG YAU BENG)

From Hong Kong comes this extraordinary pan-fried bread, made uniquely using a hot roux (a cooked flour and butter paste) that is worked into a similar dough made with cold water. The complicated process involves spreading each piece of dough with a hot oil and flour roux, and then finally rolling it up with spring onions. This is not a recipe for the faint hearted, but if you are lucky you may be offered these treats at a restaurant. The ring-shaped breads are fried in oil and have a delicious crisp outside while inside you bite into layers of soft dough around the spring onions.

SWEET BUNS (HWA JWEN)

These sweet steamed buns are a popular snack food.

PEONY BUNS

These pretty buns are often served as a sweetmeat in Hong Kong. Like *chung yau beng* they are made from two types of dough, the first made by mixing three parts wheat flour with one part root flour, and adding lard, sugar and water. A second dough, made simply from cornflour and lard, is then prepared. Both doughs are divided into 12 balls and the more elaborate dough is wrapped around the simpler one. Each ball is then rolled to a round and spread with lotus seed paste before being shaped once more into a ball. A star-shape is cut in the top of each bun and they are then deep-fried until they are crisp. The points of the star on each bun open out to create the peony shape for which the buns are named.

LEFT: Pineapple (left) and cocktail pork man to (steamed buns)

JAPANESE BREADS

There is no tradition of breadmaking in Japan. Rice was, and still is, the staple food and, until relatively recently, bread was completely unknown to all but the most travelled of the Japanese. Japan, unlike other countries in Asia, was virtually untouched by European influences until around the middle of the last century when a new philosophy was adopted and the country began to court positively the governments of Europe. Many Japanese were sent to France, Britain, Holland and Germany to see what could be learnt from the West in terms of seafaring, technology and government. Foodstuffs were probably not high on the agenda, but inevitably these Japanese visitors would have been struck by the concept of baking a food made from the flour of a grain. Recipes were taken back to Japan and very gradually more and more people acquired a liking for bread so that by the middle of this century, a few Japanese bakeries sprang up, making breads often in the image of favourite breads from Britain and France but with their own special character.

RIGHT: Melon (left) and melon and milk chocolate rolls have a soft crumb.

DOUBLE SOFT WHITE

This is a typical and extremely popular Japanese loaf, which is simply the Japanese version of an English white loaf. Indeed it is often known as "English bread" and in shape is like a tin loaf. However, the flour used by Japanese bakers is particularly soft and dense and the bread has the texture of a soft milk bread, with a similar soft smooth crust. The bread is normally cut into thick slices and then lightly toasted and eaten with butter or, more conventionally in Japan, with a spread or fruit conserve.

LEFT: Double soft white is about the most popular Japanese bread.

JAPANESE FRENCH BREAD

This is simply a French baguette, but again made with the very soft Japanese flour, so that the crumb is slightly denser and the crust less fragile than that on an authentic baguette. It can be used for sandwiches or eaten by itself with butter or a spread.

MELON BREAD

A flavoured bread, this one is popular in Britain among Japanese expatriots. The breads can be loaf-shaped but are more commonly made as rolls. Melon and milk chocolate rolls contain chunks of chocolate and are a popular tea-time bread.

JAPANESE CREAM BREAD

These small soft rolls contain cream and are consequently very soft, not unlike an English bridge roll. Like the soft white bread, these rolls are eaten at tea time with a conserve or even with butter.

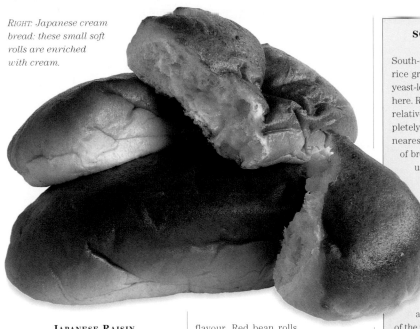

RIGHT: Japanese cream bread: these small soft rolls are enriched with cream.

SOUTH-EAST ASIAN BREADS

South-east Asia is part of the largest rice growing area of the world and yeast-leavened breads are not typical here. Rice is the staple food and until relatively recently bread was completely unknown. Rice cakes are the nearest thing to the Western idea of bread. Flat and sticky, they are usually sweetened and eaten as delicacies and sweets.

However, bread is not unheard of in South-east Asia. Western influences mean that there is now an established appetite for American and European foods and bread is becoming more popular. In Indonesia, flour mills are now springing up and much of the flour is used for bread making. One favourite white bread is called *roti tawar*. Another bread, *panada*, shows a more adventurous spirit, combining wheat flour with coconut milk. These light, sweet rolls sometimes have vegetable or meat fillings.

JAPANESE RAISIN BREAD

A simple white fruit bread, this may be tin-baked or baked in the oven so that it is evenly crusty.

JAPANESE CREAM FAIRY-TALE ROLLS

These popular tea-time rolls are filled with cream and sometimes with a mixture of chocolate and cream.

RED BEAN ROLLS

Red bean rolls are a delicious combination of ideas and flavours from countries with very different culinary backgrounds. From the outside these little bread rolls look similar to large English muffins – soft white breads with a thin, chewy crust. Inside though, these little rolls have a delicious sweet filling that is typically Japanese – red bean paste with its distinctive sweet and sour flavour. Red bean rolls are an extremely popular treat at tea time.

JAPANESE CURRY BREAD

Like red bean rolls, these are a delicious "East meets West" dish. The breads are deep fried and have a curry-flavoured filling of potatoes, with a hint of meat.

LEFT: Japanese curry bread

SHOPPING FOR BREAD AND FLOUR

The following flour mills, bakeries and foodhalls are worth visiting. Most mills sell flour direct, but it is best to telephone before visiting.

AUSTRALIA

Bowan Island Bakery
202 Lyons Road
Drummoyne
NSW 2047
Tel: (02) 9181 3524

Brown's Bakeries
PO Box 1298
Windsor
VIC 3181
Tel: (03) 9510 9520

Dallas Bread
28 Cross Street
Brookvale
NSW 2100
Tel: (02) 9905 6021

David Jones Food Hall
Cnr. Market and
    Castlereagh Streets
Sydney
NSW 2000
Tel: (02) 9266 6065

Haberfield Bakery
153 Ramsay Road
Haberfield, Sydney
NSW
Tel: (02) 9797 7715

Il Gianfornaio
414 Victoria Avenue
Chatswood, Sydney
NSW
Tel: (02) 413 4833

Infinity Sourdough Bakery
225 Victoria Street
Darlinghurst
NSW 2031
Tel: (02) 9380 4320

La Gerbe d'Or
257 Glenmore Road
Paddington, Sydney
NSW Tel: (02) 9331 10710

New Norcia Bakeries
163A Scarborough
    Beach Road
Mt Hawthorn
WA 6016
Tel: (08) 9443 9437

Quinton's Sourdough and
    Danish Shop
179 The Mall
Leura
NSW 2780
Tel: (02) 9266 6065

Victoire
285 Darling Street
Balmain
Sydney
NSW
(02) 9818 5529

Simon Johnson Purveyor of
    Quality Foods
181 Harris Street
Pyrmont
Sydney NSW 2009
NSW 2009
Tel: (02) 9552 2522

and
12–14 Saint David Street
Fitzroy
VIC 3065
Tel: (03) 9486 9456

ENGLAND

& Clarke's
122 Kensington Church
    Street
Notting Hill Gate
London W8 4BH
Tel: 0171 229 2190

Baker & Spice
46 Walton Street
London SW3 1RB
Tel: 0171 589 4734

Country Market
139–146 Golder's Green Road
London NW11 8HB
Tel: 0181 455 3289

Crowdy Mill
Bow Road
Habertonford
Totnes
Devon TQ9 7HU
Tel: 01803 732 340

Euphorium Bakery
203 Upper Street
London N1 1RQ
Tel: 0171 359 7146

Funchal Patisserie
141 Stockwell Road
London SW9 9TN
Tel: 0171 733 3134

Harrods
Food Hall
Knightsbridge
London
SW1X 7XL
Tel: 0171 730 1234

Harvey Nichols
Food Hall
109–125 Knightsbridge
London SW1X 7RJ
Tel: 0171 235 5000

Hobb's House Bakery
39 High Street
Chipping Sodbury
Bristol
BS37 6BA
Tel: 01454 321 629

and
2 North Parade
Yate
South Gloucestershire
BS37 4AN
Tel: 01454 320 890

Konditor & Cook
22 Cornwall Street
London SE1 8TW
Tel: 0171 261 0456

and
10 Stoney Street
London SE1 9AD
Tel: 0171 407 5100

Letheringsett Watermill
Riverside Road
Letheringsett
Norfolk NR25 7YD
Tel: 01263 713 153

Maison Blanc
102 Holland Park Avenue
London W11 4UA
Tel: 0171 221 2494

Mortimer & Bennett
33 Turnham Green Terrace
London W4 1RG
Tel: 0181 995 4145

Neal's Yard Bakery
6 Neal's Yard
London WC2H 9DP
Tel: 0171 836 5199

Panadam Delicatessen
2 Marius Road
London SW17 7QQ
Tel: 0181 673 4062

Pimhill Organic Centre and
    Farm Shop
Lea Hall, Harmer Hill
Nr Shrewsbury
SY4 3DY
Tel: 01939 290 075

Rushall Mill
Rushall, Pewsey
Wiltshire SN9 6EB
Tel: 01980 630 335

Sally Lunn's
4 North Parade Passage
Bath BA1 1NX
Tel: 01225 461 634

Selfridges
Food Hall
400 Oxford Street
London W1A 1AB
Tel: 0171 629 1234

Shipton Mill Limited
Long Newton
nr Tetbury
Gloucestershire GL8 8RP
Tel: 01666 505 050

The Flour Bag
Burford Street
Lechlade
Gloucestershire GL7 3AP
Tel: 01367 252 322

The Old Farmhouse
    Bakery
Steventon
nr Abingdon
Oxon OX13 6RP
Tel: 01235 831 230

Villandry Foodstore
    Restaurant
170 Great Portland Street
London W1N 5TB
Tel: 0171 631 3131

SCOTLAND

Aberfeldy Water Mill
Mill Street
Aberfeldy
Tayside PH15 2BG
Tel: 01887 820 803

Fisher and Donaldson
21 Crossgate
Cupar
Fife KY15 5HA
Tel: 01334 652 551

and
3 Church Street
St Andrews
Fife KY16 9NW
Tel: 01334 472 201

Ian Mellis
30A Victoria Street
Edinburgh EH1 2JW
Tel: 0131 226 6215

and
205 Bruntsfield Place
Edinburgh EH10 4DH
Tel: 0131 447 8889

and
492 Great Western Road
Glasgow G12 8EW
Tel: 0141 339 8998

Star Continental Bakery
158 Fore Street
Scottoun
Glasgow G14 0AE
Tel: 0141 959 7307

Taylor's of Waterside Bakery
Waterside Street
Strathaven
ML10 6AW
Tel: 01357 521 260

Valvona & Crolla
19 Elm Row
Edinburgh EH7 4AA
Tel: 0131 556 6066

Victor Hugo
26–7 Melville Terrace
Edinburgh EH9 2PR
Tel: 0131 667 1827

WALES

The Village Bakery
Melmerby Road
Melmerby
Penrith
Cumbria
CA10 1HE
Tel: 01768 881 515

Derwen Bakehouse
Museum of Welsh Life
St Fagans
Cardiff
Glamorgan
CF5 6XB
Tel: 01222 573 500

ACKNOWLEDGEMENTS

The Publishers would like to thank Jo Lethaby and Jenni Fleetwood for their skilful editing; Jill Jones, who tracked down almost all the breads; Jenny Blair for sourcing the Scottish breads; Amy Willenski, who tracked down or specially baked all the US breads; Angus Henderson and Jacky Lannel at Villandry Foodstore Restaurant, who specially baked the fougasse, épi and pane al cioccolato loaves; Christine Gough, the baker at the Museum of Welsh Life, for baking and supplying traditional Welsh breads; and Giacomo and Nuala Farruggia at Il Forno for baking and supplying many of the Italian breads, as well as the harvest loaf and hot cross buns. All recipe pictures and chapter openers are by Nicki Dowey. All other pictures are by Amanda Heywood, except for the following that have been reproduced with the kind permission of those listed: p. 124 Maison Blanc Limited; p. 9t Emma Lee/Life File; p. 8t and b e.t. archive; p. 9b English Heritage Photographic Library; p. 10t e.t. archive; p. 10b Biblioteca Estense, Modena/e.t. archive; p. 11t Andreas von Einsiedel/National Trust Photographic Library; p. 11b Eric Crichton/National Trust Photographic Library.

INDEX

NOTES

NOTES

NOTES

NOTES